HOW TO DO ADVANCED PHOTOGRAPHY

TECHNIQUES AND GUIDE ON THE BEST WAY TO GET PROFESSIONAL PICTURES

A GABRIEL PRESS

INTRODUCTION

"You don't take a photograph. You ask quietly to borrow it."
— Unknown

Photography is the quintessential universal language that does not age or lose shape. Photography is like good music. It is always in tune.

The world needs photographers to bring freedom and clarity about the chaos or beauty of the world around us.

Photographers invite us to look anew and intensely through the eyes of their cameras.

And today we look at the world through the fantastic community of photography enthusiasts.

Whether established artists or passionate about imagery, they all inform, inspire, amaze, and put the world in accurate historical context through photography.

And the present book aims to help to develop a better understanding and learning about advanced photography and is also a guide for a serious student or aspiring professional photographer.

The texts firmly explain photography in the digital era, covering the entire photographic process from a technical standpoint.

The book details the 'how' and explains the 'why's' for a complete understanding of your camera and technique.

From how cameras work to professional artmaking and theory reinforcement.

Today almost everyone can take photos with their cell phone, but is that enough to get good photos? A good picture requires high resolution, tone, color, etc.

Fortunately, it was never easier than today to take excellent photos and even become a good photographer because modern cameras with automatic modes can take care of the details to obtain fantastic photographs.

Even beginners can produce fabulous images while learning the basics and different techniques.

In this book, you will learn about those details that make a great image. Also, you will learn about the best-advanced cameras today and the difference between them.

There is information on the settings and modes of a camera for more advanced photos.

In some chapters, you will learn how to choose the appropriate software for each imaging need.

CHAPTER 1
COLOR MANAGEMENT

t's not enough to just own a camera. Everyone owns a camera. To be a photographer, you must understand, appreciate, and harness the power you hold!"
- Mark Denman

Color management helps the resolution of your original photos remain the same when reproduced on different devices. And it is a way to ensure that the consistency of color in your images or graphics in various media or devices, such as magazines, books, smartphones, etc., still is the same.

Achieving color consistency across different formats is problematic since colors pass through various methods or technologies.

So, methods used to maintain color in magazines or devices such as computer screens or smartphones are different.

Color management helps express images for devices that employ different color models, and the color model uses primarily three colors that it reproduces in a wide variety of colors.

There are two basic color models in this range of color space: the additive and the subtractive model.

RGB red, green, and blue are the most common additive color models for digital devices that can create a range of colors.

The combination of all the color ranges creates the color white.

The most common subtractive color model is CMYK for Cyan, Magenta, Yellow, and Black, used in the printing process that requires ink and is called subtractive because layers of ink inhibit white color on paper.

Different models use colored light, but colored ink RGB produces more colors than CMYK.

Through a color management system or method, a designer can create a computer graphic and reproduce the same colors in the printed form.

Through the color management method, it is possible to reproduce trees' true colors against a blue sky on a computer or printed paper.

The beauty of color management is science.

A convenient aspect of the digital format is that it is definitive.

Digital means zeros and ones, and we say it's an absolute science because every color, hue, and color variation have an exact numerical value.

On the contrary, the human body has variations. Therefore, our eyes do not see colors in the same way for everyone, and the proof is that people have different degrees of color blindness, contrary to photographic tape or a painting.

If we want to maintain consistency in the color of our images, we cannot trust our eyes.

However, color management can maintain consistency and control.

So, through this method, we can make decisions according to what is pleasing to our taste or spirit.

In photography, even though digital files have absolute values, the devices used do not display colors accurately by themselves, and it is difficult to admit it, but it is so.

However, the positive thing is that most devices only need a few adjustments to control their correct operation.

Controlling color in photography is a constant need, whether in cameras, computers, monitors, or printers.

Professional digital cameras allow you to take images in RAW or JPEG format. However, many experts differ on this decision.

JPEG will be accepted if you can show your images on the internet through a computer.

On the contrary, if you need to highlight aspects of large file sizes and obtain unique photos, it is recommended to use the RAW format that allows you to choose the color, space, and depth when exporting from RAW with a processor such as Adobe Light.

The color spectrum consists of a varied detail of colors of extreme levels.

Color profile is basically a color space, color space theoretically covers the range of millions of colors.

Every object has a color profile that, theoretically, is the color it can display.

So, one printer has one color profile, and one monitor has another, while a second printer can have a third color profile.

Printer manufacturers and monitors try to maintain consistency in color profiles.

Printers offer an RGB color space, but there are slight variations from monitor to monitor and printer to printer.

Consequently, a monitor can only display a particular range of colors which is its specific profile, although often that profile closely corresponds to a color space.

Note that a color profile includes a translator of information so that a computer can swap colors to make them more accurate when appearing on a printer or computer. So, if a laptop tends to display green color resembling blue, the color profile will try to compensate for this mixture by reinforcing the green color making it greener.

Some spaces could contain many or just a few; among those

spaces, some could be made of many blues, while others could have abundant red colors.

On the other hand, other color spaces could only contain green color.

However, the most common color spaces can be balanced and gather most of the colors people perceive because their design displays standard colors.

The discussion of color spaces usually is in practical terms.

Color space refers to a group of abstract colors like rainbow colors or colors produced by some device like a printer or smartphone.

The RGB color space is usually everywhere, as most device screens can display such a color range.

You can also occasionally find the Adobe RGB color space because most popular printers use it.

However, technically those are color profiles, not color spaces since they are no longer theoretical colors.

So, a color profile is the color space used in printers and modern devices. And how equipment interprets color information.

The color profile informs about the colors observed in color space and how those colors translate to print or display on electronic devices.

However, color space also refers to an array of abstract colors, such as the colors of the rainbow.

Color space is also an array of colors produced by equipment such as printers or the screen of a smartphone.

There are two color spaces, SRGB and Adobe RGB.

SRGB is the smallest color space.

On the other hand, Adobe RGB allows the reproduction of many more colors.

However, not all devices can display or print the full-color space of Adobe RGB.

For this reason, SRGB is more used.

For displaying images on the internet or any other screen, it is better to use SRGB color space.

In addition, the SRGB color space is compatible with almost any browser and application, which allows your image to display the resolution you expect.

The truth is that many monitors cannot reproduce Adobe RGB colors. Therefore, they cannot display the broad spectrum of Adobe RGB colors.

Browsers do not render Adobe RGB colors. Instead, they convert them to SRGB colors.

When printing, it is necessary to be careful when choosing the color space because low-end printers can only handle SRGB colors.

However, higher-end printers can work with Adobe RGB and produce better colors.

Therefore, ensure your printer or printing laboratory can use the Adobe RGB color space.

If not, using SRGB will be fine.

On your camera, you will see a button to select color space before taking a photo, and there will also be other options, including the SRGB dial on your camera.

Usually, working with SRGB is recommended.

The truth is that when shooting in RAW mode, it doesn't matter which color space is selected because RAW mode has no actual application in color space.

Once exported a photo you can apply color space, e.g., as in a JPEG file which is not very recommended.

Technically in Lightroom, you can't convert between color spaces.

Color and printing. Color profiles are not that simple because a color profile is independent of the printer and the ink and how the printer's ink interacts with the printing paper.

On the other hand, a printer plus aluminum foil paper will get a different color profile than if you use another printing paper, for example, Fine textured paper.

When using different types of paper in a printer, it will be necessary to apply the appropriate color profile to obtain the original colors.

However, using a paper type familiar to the printer will properly transfer information from the computer to the printer for a color-accurate final product.

Currently, manufacturers provide color profile combinations in their printing paper types. However, each printer varies slightly from one to another. In this case, you can create your color profile through color profile technology or a different service for color profile creation.

Unfortunately, although very aesthetic, custom color profiles still have deficiencies.

Sometimes when the resulting colors and tones are different from the expected, it can be very frustrating. Soft Proofing is the procedure that can accurately represent a digital file on a monitor before printing.

Today Soft Proofing analyzes the final artistic work and replaces the traditional hard copy proof.

Soft proofing combination permits simulating the output of printer and paper on a computer monitor.

When you apply this method to a portrait and the colors obtained are very saturated, you can desaturate them through editing before printing.

When an outdoor image is overexposed, you can still make it stand out through Lightroom's method, and then you can print it.

Now about the monitor and its calibration.

It refers to the quality of color and tone reproduced by this means.

A monitor needs calibration if you want people to see the

image resolution, how the photographer sees it on the internet, and how the photo initially looked when taken.

Likewise, you want the printed photos to match the image's resolution on the monitor. In that case, you also need to work on the color profile and test how an image will look on other devices.

A computer monitor is a sophisticated piece of equipment, and its exact calibration requires a combination of programs, for example, The X-Rite i1 Display Pro. You can use this device on more than one monitor.

A calibrated monitor can counteract unwanted shifts in color or tone.

A monitor that produces an image that is too warm can be calibrated or adjusted to produce images with cooler tones.

Warm means colors in the yellow, orange, or red spectrum, which determine an image's warmth character.

Cool means colors in the blue or violet spectrum.

Calibrating a monitor produces a color profile for that monitor so that color information interacts between the monitor, a computer, and a printer and will display more accurate colors.

CHAPTER 2
CAMERAS AND EQUIPMENT

"The painter constructs, the photographer discloses."
- Susan Sontag

Best Advanced cameras in 2023

Canon EOS R3.

Specifications.

Full model name: Canon EOS R3

Resolution:24.10 Megapixels

Sensor size:35mm

(36.0mm x 24.0mm)

Kit Lens: n/a

Viewfinder: EVF / LCD

Native ISO:100 - 102,400

Extended ISO:50 - 204,800

Shutter:1/8000 - 30 sec

Dimensions:5.9 x 5.6 x 3.4 in.

(150 x 143 x 87 mm)

Weight:35.8 oz (1,015 g)

includes batteries.

UNTITLED

Canon EOS R5.

Specifications.

45-megapixel resolution

Reproduce the most intricate of detail.

20 frames per second

Turn fleeting moments into stunning images.

Full Frame internal 8K RAW video

24/25/30p 12-bit RAW video that looks as good as real life.

Full Frame 4K/120P video

Shoot 4:2:2 10-bit high frame-rate video to enhance any creative production.

Up to 8-stop Image Stabilizer*

Shoot hand-held where you couldn't before.

ISO 100-51,200

Superb image quality, even in poor light

Built-in Wi-Fi & Bluetooth

Stay connected and send images on location.

5940 autofocus positions.

Accurate focus wherever your subject moves

CF express and SD card slots.

Maximum speed, maximum compatibility

Canon EOS 5D Mark IV

Specifications.
DSLR Sensor.
Full-frame megapixel.
45.7MPLens mount.
Nikon FLCD.
3.2in tilting touchscreen, 2.3million dots Viewfinder.
Optical Maximum continuous shooting speed.
7fpsMax video resolution.
4K
36 x 24 mm CMOS.
Effective Pixels. Approx. 30.4 megapixels.
Total Pixels. Approx. 31.7 megapixels.
Aspect Ratio. 3:2.
Low-Pass Filter. Built-in/Fixed.
Sensor Cleaning. EOS integrated cleaning system.
Colour Filter Type. Primary Colour.

Sony A9 Mark II.

Specifications.
24.2MP Full-Frame Exmor RS CMOS Sensor
BIONZ X Image Processor & Front-End LSI
693-Point Phase-Detection AF System
Up to 20 fps Shooting, ISO 100-204800
UHD 4K30p Video, Real-Time Eye AF
Blackout-Free Quad-VGA 3.7m-Dot OLED EVF
3.0" 1.44m-Dot Tilting Touchscreen LCD
5-Axis Steady Shot INSIDE Stabilization
Dual UHS-II SD Card Slots, Voice Memos
5 GHz Wi-Fi, 1000BASE-T Ethernet

Sony A1.

Specifications.
Full model name: Sony Alpha ILCE-A1
Resolution:50.10 Megapixels

Sensor size:35mm
(35.9mm x 24.0mm)
Kit Lens: n/a
Viewfinder: EVF / LCD
Native ISO:100 - 32,000
Extended ISO:50 - 102,400
Shutter:1/32000 - 30 sec
Dimensions:5.1 x 3.8 x 3.2 in.
(129 x 97 x 81 mm)
Weight:26.0 oz (737 g)
includes batteries.

Sony A7R IV

Specifications.

Type: Mirrorless Sensor: Full-frame megapixel: 61MPLens mount: Sony LCD: 3in tilting touchscreen, 1.44 million dot viewfinder: EVF, 5.76m dots Maximum continuous shooting speed: 10fpsMax video resolution: 4KUser level: Professional.

61.0MP 1 35mm full-frame Exmor R CMOS sensor and BIONZ X image processing engine.

Standard ISO 100-32000 range 3

Fast Hybrid AF with 567-point focal-plane phase-detection AF and 425-point contrast-detection AF.

High-speed continuous shooting of up to 10fps 25 with AF/AE tracking.

Nikon Z9

Specifications.

DSLR Sensor.

Full-frame megapixel.

45.7MPAutofocus.

493-point hybrid phase/contrast detect screen type.

3-inch bi-directional tilting touchscreen, 1.04m dots Maximum continuous shooting speed.

20fpsMovies: 8KUser

Effective Pixels. 45.7 million.

Sensor Size. 35.9 mm.

Image Sensor Format. FX.

Storage Media. CF express (Type B) ...

ISO Sensitivity. ISO 64–25600 in step sizes of 1/3 and 1 EV. ...

Movie. 8K UHD 7,680 × 4,320 / 30p (progressive) ...

Monitor Size. 3.2 in. ...

Monitor Type. Vertically and horizontally tilting TFT touch-sensitive LCD.

Nikon D850

Specifications.

Sensor: 45.7 MP FX BSI Sensor, 4.35μ pixel size

Sensor Size: 35.9 x 23.9mm

Resolution: 8256 x 5504

Native ISO Sensitivity: 64-25,600

Boost Low ISO Sensitivity: 32

Boost High ISO Sensitivity: 51,200-102,400

RAW Formats: 45.7 MP (Full Size), 25.6 MP (Medium Size / mRAW), 11.4 MP (Small Size / sRAW)

mRAW / sRAW File Support: 12-bit lossless compressed

Processor: EXPEED 5

Metering System: 181,000-pixel RGB Meter

Dust Reduction: Yes

Weather Sealing/Protection: Yes

Body Build: Full Magnesium Alloy

Shutter: 1/8000 – 30 seconds

Shutter Durability: 200,000 cycles, self-diagnostic shutter

Storage: 1x XQD slot and 1x SD slot (UHS-II compatible)

Viewfinder Coverage: 100%

Viewfinder Magnification: 0.75x

Speed: 7 fps, 9 fps with optional MB-D18 battery grip

Built-in Flash: No

Autofocus System: Multi-CAM 20K AF sensor.

AF Sensitivity: -4 EV at the center point

AF Detection: Up to f/8 with 15 focus points

LCD Screen: touch-enabled 3.2-inch diagonal tilting LCD with 2,359K dots

Movie Modes: 4K UHD @ 30 fps max

Slow Motion HD Video: Yes

Movie Exposure Control: Full

Movie Output: MOV, MP4

Time Lapse: 4K and 8K Timelapse

In-Camera HDR Capability: Yes

GPS: Not built-in, requires GP-1 GPS unit.

WiFi: Built-in

Illuminated Buttons: Yes

Focus Stacking Feature: Yes

Focus Peaking for Stills and Video: Yes

Wireless Radio Flash Control: Yes

Silent Photography Mode in Live View: Yes

Bluetooth: Built-in

Battery Type: EN-EN15a

Battery Life: 1840 shots (CIPA)

USB Standard: 3.0

Weight: 915g

Dimensions: 146 x 124 x 79mm

Nikon Z7 II

Specifications.

45.7MP BSI-CMOS sensor with native ISO 64

4K/60p video with 93% coverage of the sensor (a ~1.08x crop)

5-axis in-body stabilization (3-axis with adapted F-mount lenses)

10 fps burst shooting with single point AF

3.69M-dot EVF, 3.2" 2.1M-dot rear screen

-3EV focusing with F2.0 lens

1 CF Express / XQD card slot, 1 UHS-II SD card slot

New EN-EL15c battery, CIPA rated to 420 shots (LCD), 360 shots (EVF)

Compatible with new MB-N11 battery grip with vertical controls.

A good professional camera should offer quality images, accurate AF, excellent motion capture, and at least 4K videos.

The option to choose depends mainly on what you want to photograph.

If you are shooting fashion, beauty, or portraiture, a high-resolution camera will be more suitable for cropping and printing large-scale images.

If you are shooting sports or for news journalism, then a camera with excellent burst rates and tracking capability is the camera for you.

Finally, to photograph landscapes and the countryside, a waterproof camera, with lots of megapixels, will be better.

Some cameras may have many features but are very expensive, so it is best to look for a camera according to what you mainly will need.

If you regularly record video, look for a camera with features like uncropped capture, codecs (high-resolution media recording systems), and frame rates, which in this case, would be more critical than autofocus or sensor size.

UNTITLED

Equipment

To be suitably equipped in the photography business, it is necessary to have a wide variety of equipment.

The choice of cameras and lenses depends mainly on the preferred specialization practiced in photography.

Whether you want to upgrade the equipment you already have or make sure you have what you need for technique and style, let's consider the equipment and parts that are essential to have ready.

Essential professional equipment.

Filters: There are lens filters and editing filters.

Lens filters automatically adjust to the camera lens to improve image quality and protect the lens from damage.

There are three types of lens filters.

Ultraviolet filters block light waves to increase image clarity and protect the lenses.

Polarizing filters that increase contrast and remove glare from images.

Neutral density filters reduce the amount of light reaching the camera lens in excessively bright light environments.

Wireless Remote Triggers: An essential part of a professional photographer's kit has a remote control.
Some remote controls have multiple frequency channels.
A remote control is like a handy assistant, for example, when operating the button of a camera with wide angle lenses to photograph from the balcony of a church or capture aerial views of a wedding ceremony.

Tripod: Professionals use the tripod, which is necessary to frame the shoot and hold the camera steady to get a clear image.
The tripod is handy when taking long exposures.

Camera straps: Your camera is essential, and a camera strap will allow you to be ready with your camera everywhere.

Color correction card. A color correction card is handy for turning a gray photo into a good picture that can achieve a perfect color balance by wiping out the image.

Flash: A flash is an external light device connected directly to the camera that is very useful when taking photos in low light conditions.
Using a flash at events like weddings, parties, and conferences is very important.

Reflectors: A reflector or bouncer will help illuminate shadowy spaces when you must photograph outdoors, creating more balanced images.

Light kit: For studio photography, it is essential to have a lighting kit that includes soft boxes to minimize shadows,
adjustable stands, and connectors.

A lighting kit helps control the light so you can get portraits with balanced brightness.

Studio backdrop: When working in a studio, photographers use a backdrop to recreate scenes. Some are of paper or cloth.

However, you can use your creativity to build something more original.

Props: Whether your preference is to photograph people, pets, or food, it is a good idea to have some objects significantly to add color and imagination or decorate your photos, although naturally, these objects will depend on the concept in your photographs.

Monitor: Having a high-resolution calibrated monitor for previews and photo editing is crucial.

When working in the studio or correcting the color in post-production and analyzing images, a monitor is necessary to ensure you achieve artistic goals.

Editing software: An experienced photographer knows that great photos involve more than pressing a button, which is why professionals retouch their images using software like Adobe Lightroom and Photoshop.

Photoshop is excellent for effects and editing photos in more detail, while Lightroom is better for quickly and easily fine-tuning details and organizing photo files.

External hard drives: Hard drives are essential tools for professional photographers because, over the years, many photos accumulate that need to be preserved in storage devices to export them to different memory devices later to save and use when required.

Camera Bag: A good quality camera bag is essential to carry all the necessary equipment to each shooting location.

Business Equipment Protection: Investing in cameras and professional photographic equipment can be a significant expense.

Often the locations you work in photography range from shooting in the studio to shooting in the field.

Naturally, your equipment can be at risk of damage, so it's a good idea to protect it with commercial protection insurance.

CHAPTER 3
ADVANCED CAMERA SETTINGS

"If you can see it, you can shoot it."
   - Ted Grant

There are many possibilities to maneuver the camera settings, but to get the best images is necessary to pay attention to the most critical camera settings.

Camera mode (allowing manual control)

Camera modes, in P, S, A, M. Tv, and Av these controls are enough to control the settings of a camera, if the camera is not in fully automated mode.

If you are uncomfortable with the aperture selection, it is best to shoot in P or A/Av programmed auto or aperture priority.

Use A/Av to select the aperture to improve the depth of field.

You can create a familiar starting point by resetting the camera; there is no recommendation for this.

Or, for example, set exposure compensation for a brighter or darker photo.

If you don't select something else in the camera, your next photo will have the same exposure you set previously, even if you haven't taken a picture for days.

Please familiarize yourself with your camera's settings and how to reset them.

Most cameras offer default settings that you can call upon in a pinch.

Another critical camera setting is the focal length, which chooses the angle and gives perspective, plus it has two effects on photos.

When shooting a telephoto, the focal length is approximately 180mm.

In Light Telephoto, Focal Length is 70 mm.

In Wide Angle, Focal Length 25 mm.

All these three lengths are (35mm equivalent)

The focal length determines the width of an image section, so you can get more of the image by zooming in.

Suppose you take three photos from the same spot in a few minutes. The three focal lengths will create different image content and composition possibilities without using extremely wide-angle or telephoto.

The focal length determines the perspective and proportions in a picture which is its primary role.

Focal length is critical for image composition, effects in pictures, and expression possibilities.

So instead of using the zoom slider, get closer and shoot with a wide-angle focal length.

The primary function of autofocus is to provide excellent sharpness when the lenses are at a reasonable distance.

All modern camera technology and settings aim to ensure that your camera can quickly and reliably find an optimal distance, even in low light conditions.

The resolution will be good when the autofocus works at an average distance.

If the subject is far away, direct the autofocus manually and set the autofocus to the part of the image you want to focus.

Continuously adjust the distance, whether you're focusing once, still, or following a moving subject.

The camera's three main settings are Aperture, shutter speed, and ISO. They control the recording of incident light which is the essence of the art of photography.

Each of these settings has a particular effect on how an image looks. Each effect results in exposure and how light or dark can appear in a snap.

Aperture's effect on an image is a more precise depth of field.

Exposure time controls motion blur and camera shake.

ISO sensitivity controls noise.

Set the aperture, shutter speed, and ISO manually on your camera for exposure control.

Your camera's automatic exposure meters measure the brightness of incident light.

Ways to adjust exposure.

Exposure lock: In this function, you can reframe the scene but prevent a current exposure from changing.

This function also allows you to keep the same brightness in each shot.

Exposure Compensation: In this setting, you can manually correct for a bright or dark exposure; however, this deviates from automatic exposure metering.

It is also helpful to select different types of exposure metering, and there are three possible exposure combinations, although there is no specific rule for best results.

However, the result of exposure metering is a combination of the three main settings: aperture, exposure, and ISO sensitivity.

White balance or color contribution is a setting that corrects and adds color to pictures when colors are warmer or more relaxed.

The camera procedure is automatic or manual.

Advanced or beginner, the decision to use flash or not is yours for an extra dose of light.

Flash can be balanced with the exposure time, especially to

control the brightness of the image's background with longer exposures.

The file format RAW is more complex than the standard JPG created by the camera.

Using either depends on your expectations and skill level in a shooting situation.

Shooting in RAW format may give better results, but this format needs heavy processing, particularly in brightening and darkening images.

On the other hand, light editing isn't much of a problem in JPG format besides post-editing isn't such a big reason to shoot in RAW.

CHAPTER 4
CHOOSING LENSES

"**P**hotographs are just light and time."
- Aza Holmes

Lens and aperture.

Aperture: The maximum aperture on all lenses indicates the amount of light a lens can allow to pass to the sensor.

Abundant light allows shooting in relatively dark conditions without blurring the image due to movement.

The degree of the aperture is indicated by numbers, for example, F/2.8 or (1:2.8)

When the degree or aperture number is smaller, more light enters the camera.

In theory, the ideal aperture would be an objective equal to 1, although, in practice, the brightest lenses offer a maximum aperture of F/1.2 and F/3.2.

The higher the aperture number, the less the lens is worth.

Only telephoto lenses offer high aperture numbers.

Zoom lenses typically use two aperture numbers (F/2.8 - F/5.6)

Smaller aperture numbers indicate the amount of light admitted at a wider angle.

The large aperture numbers indicate the amount of light allowed into the lens with maximum zoom.

The focal length is the most important when choosing lenses,

When selecting lenses is very important to consider the focal length established in millimeters.

Also, the specifications show if the lens is of wide angle or telephoto.

Wide-angle or zoom lenses have pros and cons.

Telephoto lenses have a view of very distant objects, and they also are preferred for portraits because of their ability to reveal facial proportions better than a wide-angle lens.

However, telephoto lenses produce more blurred backgrounds due to their shallower depth of field than wide-angle lenses.

Telephoto lenses also have lower brightness, plus camera shake while taking the photo can cause blurred backgrounds.

Telephoto lenses are also usually larger than wide-angle lenses.

However, when you want a better capture of the landscape, wide-angle lenses are better for nature photography.

Also, this type of lens offers a brighter depth of field and is smaller than telephoto lenses.

The downside of wide-angle lenses is that they could be more suitable for photographing people in a portrait photography context.

Wide-angle lenses give the impression of a more considerable distance between near and far objects making a model look like it has a more prominent nose or other features such as eyes.

Another peculiarity of wide-angle lenses is that straight lines tend to curve at the edges of the image.

The combination of the qualities of both lenses, wide angle and telephoto, results in the so-called standard lenses that allow us to see our environment as our eyes see it concerning distance and size.

For the focal-length lens of 135 millimeters or telephoto format, the standard lens is 50 millimeters.

Any lens with a smaller focal length is known as a wide-angle lens, and lenses with a longer focal length are called telephoto lenses.

Telephoto lenses are ideal for photographing people and pets, landscape and street photography, and product photography.

Standard 3x zoom compact cameras have a focal length ranging from 35mm to 105mm, consistent with the 135mm format.

Typically, the focal length depends on the size of the camera's image sensor, which means that the lens's focal length is different on each camera.

The focal length is equivalent to the so-called full frame of a DSLR camera.

There are essential differences between the fixed and zoom lens.

With zoom lenses, you can get several focal lengths, and this type of lens has two specific focal lengths, for example, 18-55 mm, indicating the lens's zoom range.

On compact cameras, this is equivalent to a 3x zoom.

The advantages of fixed lenses are that they are smaller and lighter and offer better brightness than zoom lenses.

Another quality of prime lenses is that image errors are more acccssible to correct than with zoom lenses.

Depending on the price of the lens and the manufacturer's brand, fixed lenses offer better image quality.

There are SLR cameras that use different sizes of image sensors, which confuses the actual capability of a telephoto or wide-angle lens.

The most common attempt is to convert a focal length to a full-frame equivalent.

An example is a full frame sensor less Canon SLR camera in which the crop factor is 1.6, which means you must multiply the focal length by 1.6 to determine what the 135mm format would be in full frame.

A range of 18-55 would be roughly equal to 29.88mm.

Nikon – 1.5

Canon – 1.6

Pentax – 1.5

Sony – 1.5

Major manufacturers continue to work on image stabilization in the lens of DSLR cameras.

Stabilization in the lens consists of moving the elements to eliminate camera shake.

Brands that provide built-in image stabilization in their lenses are, for example, Nikon-VR, Canon-IS, Pentax, Sigma-OS, Tamron-VC.

Color refractive correction in photography is closely related to light.

One challenging aspect for lens manufacturers is that light has strange abilities, such as different light colors taking on a different curvature when passing through a camera lens.

This phenomenon leads to color changes, especially at the edges of an image, and to counter this effect, researchers use a technique called low dispersion glass.

Nikon – ED (extra-low dispersion)

Pentax – ED (extra-low dispersion)

Sigma – APO (Lens made of special glass with anomalous partial dispersion)

Tamron – LD (hybrid lens element that reduces aspherical and chromatic aberration)

Another error in camera lenses is distortion.

When straight lines toward the edges of an image curve either in or out.

Some lens manufacturers provide indications that the lenses are distortion corrected.

Pentax – AL (Aspherical Lenses)

Sigma-ASP (spherically ground lens elements, to correct possible lens aberrations)

Tamron-AD (anomalous dispersion)

Some lenses can correct perspective or Focus Shift, and they also offer the option of changing the plane of focus to manipulate the depth of field, although this type of lens is rarely used.

Nikon-PC (Perspective Control)

Canon-TS (measurement of how much light is going through the lens at any given f-stop)

Digital image sensors in SLR cameras have smaller areas than traditional negatives, and now lenses are smaller and lighter. However, these lenses are incompatible with DSLR full-frame image sensors or conventional film cameras.

Nikon–DX (refers to the size of its image sensor)
Canon – EF-S (Electro-focus short back focus)
Pentax–DA (Daguerrotipe)
Sony–DT (Digital (D) technology)
Sigma–DC (Defocus Control)
Tamron–DI-II (Digitally integrated

There are lenses for full-frame image sensors available and used on regular film SLRs.

Nikon – Lenses do not have the mark DX (refers to the size of its image sensor)
Canon – EF (Electronic Focus)
Pentax – FA (Factory Automation)
Sigma – DG (lens designed for a Full Frame camera)
Tamron – DI (Digital intermediate)

. . .

Macro, a characteristic of compact cameras, they can get very close to subjects and take pictures of small things, insects, and flowers, etc.

Nikon–Micro
   Canon–Macro
   Sigma–Macro
   Tamron–Macro

CHAPTER 5
ADVANCED EXPOSURES

"What do we feel when we look at a good photograph? We just want to be there, right at the exact moment that photo taken!"
- Mehmet Murat Ildan

Control of light levels.

Modern cameras use reflective light meter measurements to achieve the correct aperture and shutter speed at a given ISO.

A reflective meter measures the intensity of the light that bounces off the photographed subject.

The meter measures the light after hitting the subject and determines how reflective an object is for a proper exposure setting, allowing the photographer to manually interpret the information to set the shutter speed and aperture.

The light meter compares the hue and not the color of a photographic scene so that red colors will register as slightly dark instead of gray tones as a combination of a black and white.

The meter tells you to expose a photo to a mid-tone of around 18 percent gray or darker.

Some scenes, like snow, white dresses, and shadowed backgrounds, are far from 18 percent gray and confuse the camera's meter.

Modern cameras use three different metering systems that balance the diversity of scene lighting.

Each system offers different results depending on the scene.

The spot meter helps to read the light levels on specific elements of the image.

Center-weighted meter mode sits halfway between matrix and partial, metering large dots in the camera's viewfinder.

Usually, people use the center of image metering on DSLR cameras.

Your camera owner's manual provides details on this.

SLR cameras have four main metering shooting modes: Manual, Aperture Priority, Shutter Priority, and Program.

Manual mode gives you control to set shutter speed and aperture based on light reading analysis, giving you control and allowing you to get bright and dark elements.

So, depending on what you are exposing, you can explore manual mode.

The other modes are auto or semi-auto modes, but they are different and separate from autofocus.

In automatic mode, the camera controls the exposure and makes the decisions.

However, shooting in manually with a spot meter will result in excellent photos.

Tips to go beyond the basics of long-exposure photography.

(ND filter is a physical filter made of resin or glass that attaches to the front of the lens.

Film or digital cameras use ND filters. They can block out some of the light in the image.

If a specific area in the image is too bright and you wish to correct it, an ND filter may be the solution).

#1 – Use ND filters for long daytime exposures as a dark landscape technique. But to avoid missing out on some fantastic shoots, don't overuse them.

With the right equipment, daylight scenes can be great for long exposures.

Neutral density filters can block light, allowing a slow shutter speed without overexposing the shot.

With the graduated version of filters and polarizers, neutral density filters are among the three filters worth having in a camera bag.

Lighter filters, like ND2, don't affect an image much.

However, by using an ND filter or higher, you can create long exposures in daylight, and with a set of ND filters, you can take long exposures without creativity limitations.

#2: For long-exposure photography, shoot subjects that are a bit out of the ordinary, like anything that moves predictably.

For starters, the clouds, the tide, or a light breeze over the tall grass.

You can photograph stars or any moving light source using long-exposure photography techniques.

Slow shutter speeds also go beyond the norm and create motion blur.

The combination of ND filter and prolonged exposure emphasizes contrast, like a sunrise or sunset, and allows you to capture a ray of light in near darkness.

#3 Cover your camera to prevent light leaks because while experimenting with long exposures, light can enter the camera through the viewfinder and cause bright spots in the image.

Most long-exposure photographers cover their cameras to prevent light leaks by taping the viewfinder or placing a cloth over the camera as a light leak solution.

#4: To avoid waiting too long to see the results of your long exposure session, you can do a quick test by taking a photo with a shorter shutter speed but carefully balancing it with a higher ISO.

Remember that each stop of light doubles or halves the amount of light. Remember to set ISO and shutter speed at the same number of settings stops, and with the same exposure, take a shorter shutter speed test to check your long-exposure photography quickly.

Suppose you take a five-minute exposure at f/8 and ISO 100. And you shot at ISO 3200; That's a five-stop difference (200, 400, 800, 1600, 3200) because you doubled the ISO five times. Most cameras set the shutter speed to 1/3 of a stop, so you can click 15 shutter speeds to get five stops of light; in this example, that is ½. So, at ½ second, f/8 and ISO 3200 will produce the same exposure as a five-minute photo, f/8 ISO 100. If you're not comfortable with numbers, download an exposure calculator app.

Choose the one for IOS or the one for Android.

Determining what shutter speed to use in a long exposure shot requires experimentation. Still, on the other hand, a five-minute exposure is good when creating effects on clouds or waves and even longer for slower-moving objects.

For a photography list to be complete, it needs to include exposure stacking, which is an excellent shooting and editing technique that allows for longer exposure time and the use of fewer ND filters.

With this technique, the shooter decides how much motion blur he wants after taking the shots.

With prolonged exposures, there is the risk of allowing a lot of noise into images, whether using a low ISO or not.

More megapixels in Modern cameras make image noise worse; however, new cameras have a design that reduces the sensor overheating, which causes image noise.

When shooting a stacked exposure, first proceed as for a regular long exposure (with tripod and remote release), then divide the shot into multiple shorter exposures, five one-minute images instead of one five minutes long image.

Then stack the image together, and you'll get the effect of just one total exposure time of the shots combined.

After taking your shots, open Photoshop and look for the files (Scripts). Load files to Stacks and select the files to combine.

Check the two boxes at the bottom, "one for automatically aligning and the other for creating intelligent objects). Next, go to Layer (smart objects -stack mode). This mode creates a blur effect like a long exposure.

Then proceed with standard post-processing.

Excellent long-exposure photography requires more than just a few pieces of equipment or an understanding of shutter speed.

However, practice makes perfect, so apply long exposure advice like exposure stacking and ND filters, and you'll get extraordinary images.

CHAPTER 6
ADVANCED FOCUS TECHNIQUES

"Photography, to me, is catching a moment which is passing, and which is true."
- Jacques-Henri Lartigue

Photography focus is very important, and sometimes, you just need to point your camera at a subject you want to photograph, but sometimes you won't get the desired results.

However, there are camera focus techniques that will help you get some blur at a specific point in an image or have an utterly sharp picture.

Shooting to landscape or when subjects are motionless is relatively easy.

But it is challenging when trying to shoot action or sports photography.

And focusing on the viewfinder takes more work.

On the other hand, focusing on a digital viewfinder works better because the viewfinder can zoom into the details, and the focused area can have a blue halo that helps to identify distance.

If there is no manual technique, autofocus can help, but you need to know a few methods.

The AF functionality is quite simple.

With the camera in AF mode, press the shutter button halfway and watch your subject come into sharp focus in the viewfinder, and for some situations, this is adequate.

However, modern DSLR cameras come with many more modes and settings. Also, their AF systems come tuned to various shooting scenarios, and the AF system camera mode determines how you maintain focus.

If a photographer is unfamiliar with selecting camera settings for types and situations of subjects, they probably won't use the full potential of the AF system.

AF's three main modes are auto-servo, single-servo, and continuous-servo.

Auto-Servo or AF-A mode. This mode automatically selects single or continuous mode, but first, the AF system determines whether the subject is stationary or moving.

However, more advanced photographers use it at a minimal level.

Single-servo mode, AF-S, is the mode in which the AF system focuses the lens on the selected point and locks the captured focus distance.

Typically, the camera disables the shutter release in this mode until the lens has focused. At the same time, the lens won't perform focus tracking.

Ideally, this mode offers better results on static subjects.

If you keep the shutter button pressed halfway, the focus distance will not change; however, you can recompose the image since an AF point will not cover the subject.

Make sure the distance between the camera and the subject stays the same before taking the photo, and you will get a clear image.

Otherwise, it will be necessary to refocus.

Continuous servo or AF-C In this mode, the AF system continuously focuses on the selected covered area while constantly monitoring the focus distance.

If the distance between the camera and the subject changes, the focus is adjusted automatically.

This mode is excellent for moving subjects as the AF system will alter focus by following the moving subject, plus the shutter can be released at any time, even if the objective is not focused.

While the AF mode lens focuses, the shooter can simultaneously press the shutter button.

In AF-C mode as soon as the system detects a moving subject.

It will activate its focus tracking through a predictive function that uses information from the system to adjust the focus point to the subject's position.

During the delay from the camera's reflection, the shots happening in a swift sequence will be the felt sensation.

In AF-C Mode, the camera is constantly adjusting the focus. Therefore, it is necessary to lock the focus distance by pressing the (AF-L) button to take a photo without the AF point covering the subject.

Using AF-C, use the lowest aperture value (F/1.8 to F/4) so that your subject appears sharp, but the background is blurred.

For any AF system to work correctly, two conditions must be present.

There must be some variation around the subject in focus first because a continuous tone will not work in a light stable condition area.

Second, the conditions require a significant amount of light for autofocus to work well.

Therefore, in certain low-light conditions, autofocus may not work.

When the cameras autofocus is on, it constantly searches for an image subject on which to focus.

When either condition is present, the focus will attempt to look at an image.

In part, the numerical distribution, and types of autofocus of the camera determine the accuracy of autofocus.

The primary spread of a DSLR camera can be as little as three AF points, while some professional models can have up to 60 autofocus points. However (AF-S) is very handy in landscape or street photography, especially when traveling.

In some cases, using AF-C may be essential, such as photographing horse racing, kitesurfing, windsurfing, and other sports where unpredictable movement occurs.

Autofocus areas are another essential photographic concept, and this concept determines which AF points to use.

The three main AF points differ slightly due to the make of the camera.

These points are the single point, multiple point, and automatic point.

In single-point focus, known as manual AF point by Canon and single-point AF-area mode by Nikon, you select the individual AF point.

So, the camera does not influence the AF point you choose.

Often the center AF point is the most reliable.

However, when it comes to composition, it's often best to place your subject in the middle of the frame, and if you're taking a picture where the image subject is off-center, position the center AF point over your subject.

For control, lock the focus before recomposing or selecting the AF point in the desired area.

Multi-point mode is a variation of single-point mode in which the AF system uses the individual AF point initially selected by the shooter.

However, the subject must not move from the area covered by the AF point.

When a subject leaves the covered area, the AF system evaluates information from a preselected number of surrounding AF points to maintain focus on the moving subject.

The number of autofocus points varies depending on the camera model.

Multi-point mode is a good option when shooting motion.

However, supporting a selected AF point depends on the number of AF points used.

Supported autofocus points must not extend beyond the subject's edges, or the AF system will focus on another part of the background.

Therefore, selecting a few AF points in a support group reduces the data a camera must process, increasing focusing speed and accuracy.

Dynamic-area autofocus, or auto-point mode is a point-and-shoot AF solution. This mode is fully automated and prioritized for identifying skin tones and all features of the human face.

The focus will prioritize those closest to the camera if multiple faces are in the frame.

When the scene contains multiple elements with a similar color tone, the auto-point mode will not correctly work as the focus will mainly capture other aspects than the ones intended.

AF-L lock button. In single-servo autofocus (AF-S) mode, the focus distance locks in as soon as the camera acquires focus and, if necessary, allows you to recompose an image before the shutter is released as long as the shutter release stays half-pressed.

While in continuous mode (AF-C), the focus distance constantly adjusts while the shutter-release button is halfway pressed, so the lens focuses on the scene selected by the AF point.

When recomposing the photo, AF-C can mess things up and cause the lens to blur, resulting in a blurry image.

However, an alternative technique is to use the (AF-L) lock function, which disables activation of the AF system from the shutter release.

The AF-L button acts as an on/off switch for AF mode.

To lock the focus distance, press and hold the button (AF-C stops working)

Release the button to return to AF-C mode again.

Once focus is gained via AF-S, press the AF-L button to lock focus so you can freely recompose without worrying about the AF system changing the focus distance.

Focus Shift: For example, some of the uses and procedures for working in this mode are on display on the Nikon D850's camera designed for dark environments thanks to its backlit buttons, excellent low light autofocusses, and high ISO noise maneuverability.

Focus shifting on this camera is primarily used to produce images for focus stacking combined with third-party software to create final images with a maximum depth of field.

With a single photo, we don't have to worry about getting a great depth of field, but we can consider how we can adjust the aperture to obtain high-resolution images with each shot.

So, we must consider the aperture at which the lens works best.

In focus shift mode, the camera can take a series of shots from a selected focus position to infinity.

You can choose an initial focus position either in front of or slightly close to a subject section point for the desired depth of field.

There is a choice of ten focus step widths, and the amount of focus distance changes with each shot. And focus distance is not determined solely by one factor but by a variety of data from the lens, including focal length and aperture.

However, when choosing the focus step width, selecting the range number 5 or even less is best to prevent areas in the focus-stacked image from being out of focus.

Focus shift photography is relatively easy, and it is advisable if you want to print large images with a focus step width of 2 or 3.

You can set multiple photo shots to values between 1 and 300.

Typically, more than a hundred shots can cover a selected depth of field if the subject is an insect or other small objects when shooting macro at the described settings with an aperture of f/5.6. And step width of 2 or 3.

However, to photograph a nearby landscape that stretches into the distance, only a few shots are needed, using a wide-angle lens, keeping in mind that the depth of field of individual photos is already deep enough.

Focus shift photography is practiced primarily with still subjects and the camera on a tripod.

You can choose silent photography or use the traditional mechanical shutter.

The camera folder menu has the options New Folder and Reset File Numbering.

After shooting, performing focus stacking is quicker if the photos in each focus shift series are in numbered folders.

Look in the focus shift shooting menu to set the width of the focus step.

Disable functions that may interfere with focus shift photography operations.

When the camera shooting can't start, it's probably because the focus setting for that function is unavailable.

Therefore, insert a memory card before adjusting the settings, which may fix the problem.

CHAPTER 7
THE BRENIZER METHOD

"The art of photography is all about directing the attention of the viewer."
- Steven Pinker

"The biggest cliche in photography is sunrise and sunset."
- Catherine Opie

The Brenizer method is a photographic technique that creates digital images that exhibit a shallow depth of field and a wide angle of view and is also a technique designed to capture fantastic pictures with minor equipment.

The concept is simple and involves taking a series of shallow depth-of-field images using a telephoto lens.

Then move the lens slightly after each shot and stitch the images together to create a panoramic view.

Panoramic photographers typically shoot landscapes, cityscapes, and interiors.

It is not possible to create a shallow depth of field effect with a wide-angle lens because the longer the focal length, the greater the depth of field, so to capture a shallow depth of field image at 24mm, you need to get very close to the subject, but that would ruin the wide-angle look.

However, the Brenizer method emphasizes the amount of background blur and depth of field in each area of view, and the best way to achieve this is to stand close to the subject of the photo and photograph it with a fast lens wide open.

Use a 50mm f/.4 for a wider angle of view and an 85mm f/1.4 to emphasize background blur.

Class lenses work fine, like 35mm f71.4. 50mm f/1.8. 85mm f/2.

The process for using this photographic method is relatively simple. However, it would help if you kept in mind some caution when practicing this method.

Preview your final image composition, so you know what to cover only and what parts of the image you need to crop.

It would be best if you shot a bit more than you'll need, and you may find taking vertical snippets easier, though horizontal snippets are more accessible to track.

Also, avoid leaving too many gaps, as they can become a whitespace. And once you stitch the panorama, you may need to over-crop or discard your image altogether because of too many blank spaces.

Once the lens is focused, lock the shutter speed, aperture, white balance, and JPG settings.

When switching to manual focus and M exposure, some prefer to focus with the AF button rather than the shutter release button while in M mode to prevent the exposure and focus from shifting as they move around the frame.

Overlapping the panorama by 30 to 50 percent will make stitching easier for your software. Still, excess images will result in more stitches that will eventually need correction by removing unnecessary images.

Start with your topic, cover it first and move systematically, keeping in mind the areas already covered.

Capturing the subject first is better and more if your subject is people.

Shooting with wide-open lenses can lead to vignetting that can ruin the results.

However, when processing images in Lightroom 4, you can remove vignetting using the Lens Correction tab before stitching your final panorama together.

Stitching more than 50 images can take time, depending on your computer's power, and panoramas made from just a few photos can look amazing. Also, due to parallax, straight lines are often hard to handle.

To keep the lines straight, remove lens distortion in the lens correction tab.

When taking group portraits with this technique, the resulting images may show significant curvature of the field of focus.

So, to get less camera shake, it's better to keep the distance by using longer lenses.

You can use the Brenizer method in several situations, such as when you need a wide angle of view and shallow depth of field, but you can also experiment with it while making it work for your unique needs.

With the Brenizer method, Photoshop CS5 software works well, but it takes a bit of time to work with it.

However, to get great results, you must master the technique first, so back up your critical shots with regular captures and downsize before stitching.

In addition to Photoshop CS5, other similar software is available specifically for panoramic stitches.

The benefits of the Brenizer method include creating unique effects, and high-resolution portrait subject files optimized for an enlarged print.

The method requires only a camera and a telephoto lens; even a tripod is not a requirement.

The drawbacks can be that depending on the number of shots,

it can take time to capture a single image and longer to edit and combine files in Photoshop.

Also, a change in light can affect the effect, but above all, it is the time spent in the process.

Step 1.

Look carefully at a photo opportunity. Technically any subject composition will do. However, it's best to look for layers to create an effect that matches a shallow depth of field.

Step 2.

Although not necessary, a tripod can be helpful, and when your area of work is ready, identify your composition and get closer to your subject to increase the effect of a shallow depth of field.

Set your camera to Manual mode, and then check the following settings.

Aperture: Shoot at the maximum width of your lens. Width ranges can be f/1.2, f/4, and f/5.6. The wider the camera aperture will result in a better effect.

ISO and Shutter Speed: ISO at its base value if light conditions are good, choose the shutter speed based on exposure criteria, and in dim light, increase the ISO for a brighter exposure and faster shutter speed.

White Balance: Manual mode would be better, but you can also choose a white balance preset.

Focal length: 100mm, but the focal length should remain the same on every shot, and using a prime lens will make this easier, as the zoom lens will need handling to be very carefully, and if there is movement, the focal lens will need adjustment.

Focus: After focusing your subject, switch to manual mode and don't change the setting until finishing shooting.

Step 3.

Organize your layout shooting.

Your composition and focal length determine the number of images you take; some shooters take around 20-50 files.

While shooting, try to follow an order and avoid photo shooting randomly.

Stage 4.

Batch edit your files using software like Lightroom.

Adjust white balance, exposure, contrast, and saturation, syncing all your images, each file with the same edit.

If you want, you can add complex editing to the final photo.

Finally, export your images to a stitching program like Photoshop or another.

Depending on how many images you want to merge, it's best to export your photos as JPEG files between 700 and 1000 pixels.

Step 5.

Combine images.

Now stitch your photos together in panorama style.

If you use Photoshop, go to Auto Photomerge, then check Blend Images Together, select Auto Layout, find your images, and press ok.

Depending on the size of the files, the joining process can take a few minutes or even half an hour.

The software would present your photos in a lovely arrangement if you did your shooting in an organized layout.

Then you only need to crop your image, and now you can save it as a JPEG file.

CHAPTER 8
TONE IN PHOTOGRAPHY

"Contrast is what makes photography interesting."
    - Conrad Hall

While there are many things to consider when taking photos, such as lighting, composition, and color, another important aspect of photography is tone.

The tone differs between the lightest and the darkest area in a photograph.

A camera sometimes needs clarification when it assumes that the average shade of 18 percent grey is standard in every image.

Eighteen percent grey is like a photography norm, which is why sometimes you are unsatisfied with a photo that may look right.

A black object in the dark consists of dark tones, and the same object in the snow consists of light tones, so the camera will dodge or burn the same thing trying to turn it into an 18 percent shade of grey.

A dark tone is a shaded area in a photo. The light image tone is the bright area.

Human eyes can distinguish the range of tones in a scene and detail in bright and deep dark areas. Still, a camera lens can't do this automatically.

Hence, the camera assumes that the average hue across the entire image is 18 percent.

Turning the image to black and white and then blurring it will create the overall photo tone.

When a camera corrects an exposure in auto mode, it only creates the same average gray image tone of 18 percent.

Typically, when shooting in auto mode, the camera measures the light reaching the subject by managing the exposure, allowing the correct amount of light to pass through the lens onto the sensor.

In contrast, the camera program will organize the darkness and brightness tone of the photo.

However, the camera will need clarification and will not cooperate when trying to get the moody gray sky over a dark landscape because the camera program constantly tries to reproduce the standard 18 percent mid-grey average tone.

With the correct exposure, the black-and-white gamut and details in the photo will appear crystal clear.

Overexposure: When too much light hits the sensor, the resulting image will be too white or too bright.

Underexposure: When insufficient light hits the camera sensor, the image will be too dark.

When shooting in auto mode, a photo will invariably appear with an average 18 percent gray tone.

By deactivating the automatic mode, you can manage how much light hits the sensor and thus avoid the standard grey tone.

Setting a different size aperture in the shutter speed and ISO will give you unique hues in your pictures.

. . .

Tonal photography definitions.

The tonal range is the difference between bright and dark, and it can be affected due to the shooting location and post-production process, especially by some software like Photoshop.

Photographers generally want to render realistic scenes using a wide tonal range.

And there's room to push the boundaries in high-low key and abstract lighting.

Some post-production techniques, such as the tone curve, work well to adjust exposure, temperature, de-haze, contrast, and shadows.

You can try other tools and find the ones that work best for you; for example, to work on specific areas of a photo by taping and dodging, use Photoshop.

When possible, work with the raw file format.

A great way to practice the tonal range technique is to shoot in black and white and work with various shades of gray.

The split-tone method adds color to the highlights and shadows separately to black and white photography, simultaneously allowing color adjustment in specific parts of the image.

So, working with black and white split toning adds new nuances to the shadows and highlights of your photos.

Some combinations are brown/orange, reddish/brown with blue color, or even others.

High-tone or "high-key" photography is more than dodging images, brightening shadows, or diminishing highlights in a photo.

But instead, a high tone or subject matter creates emotion or extremely delicate light.

In addition, the positive space refers to areas of paramount interest in a photograph and deals with the compositional elements influenced by different aspects of the composition.

To start working with tones in high-tone photography, try well-lit environments, including dark elements that have some contrast but avoid too much brightness.

Cool tones in photography add a slight blue or purple cast to an image and, depending on the subject and composition, impart emotions to color and monochrome images that suggest sadness and tranquility.

Blue hour is ideal for cool-tone photography, with the white balance set to fluorescent or tungsten white light.

Use on-camera lighting rigs with blue or purple filters and adjust color and temperature sliders in post-production.

So, when considering tone in your shots, engage both hemispheres of your brain.

Practice post-production tools and analyze the emotional components of your photographic work for uniqueness and creativity.

Hue or tone is powerful and sets the mood of a final image, and there are many ways to achieve those unique tones.

Use lighting of different color temperatures or outdoor lighting with colored filters.

Editing software can also deepen the tones in an image, and it's essential to know the touch tones add to your photos, both in color and black and white photography, so that you can choose the right ones.

In black-and-white photography, the tones change to sepia and white. However, color photography is about enhancing the image's mood and purpose.

To think in tones is to think of warm and cool colors and their properties.

Warm colors like red, yellow, orange and brown bring feelings and emotions to an image.

Cool colors like green and purple tend to bring about refreshing feelings, but blue often brings up feelings of sadness.

As mentioned, tones in monochrome photography tend to be more prominent, and there are three ways to add style to black and white photos; One way is to add color to the lighter parts of an image while keeping the black areas black.

In color photography, there are a few options; for example, sepia can soften an image and make it look old-fashioned.

Another way to tone monochrome photos is by using Selenium, which adds drama through its blue-purple hue.

Gold with its orange-red effect with bluish-toned blacks.

Cyanotypes provide a deep blue hue that replicates the glass plate process.

The main concern with tone is the overuse of these techniques; however, other times, a hue in your photo is all you need to impact an image.

However, feel free to experiment to find what works best for your creativity.

CHAPTER 9
IMAGE SENSORS

"One advantage of photography is that it's visual and can transcend language."
- Lisa Kristine

The image sensor receives incoming light through the shutter speed in a digital camera, then converts the light into an electrical signal which the camera analyzes and translates the data into color.

The quality of photos depends on many factors, and one of those factors is the size of the digital sensor.

However, there are pros and cons when selecting a sensor's size, so the best is to know which one works best for your photographic needs.

A camera's sensor determines the quality of a photograph, affecting things like depth of field, dynamic range, low-light performance, and the resolution of the entire image.

There are two main types of sensors in a camera, CCD, and CMOS.

. . .

CCD (charge-coupled device). The quality of this sensor lies in its high resolution with low noise and good dynamic range.

However, these sensors consume much more power than CMOS, commonly used in medium-format cameras.

CMOS (complementary metal oxide semiconductor). This type is more common than CCD sensors, uses less power, and is excellent in high-speed burst shooting mode.

A weakness of this sensor is its lower sensitivity to light and more grain, although it is cheaper to produce.

How the size of a sensor impacts the different elements of an image are diverse, and one of these is the resolution that depends on the number of megapixels the sensor has.

Resolution: A camera sensor contains millions of (photosites) that capture light.

At the same time, light translates into pixels, and one million of these pixels equals one megapixel.

Therefore, the larger sensor can hold enormous (photosites), and more megapixels result in a higher image resolution.

Depth of field: The distance in an image where objects show an acceptable level of sharpness when focused.

When factors such as the camera's aperture, focal length, and subject distance are equal, a larger sensor will show a shallower depth of field, and a larger sensor requires the camera to be closer to the subject to fill the frame. Or use a more extended focal length.

Equivalently, a camera with a smaller sensor will present a greater depth of field.

An SLR or mirrorless camera with a full-frame sensor provides more flexibility regarding the depth of field.

. . .

Low-light performance: Compared to a small sensor, a larger sensor contains larger photosites allowing a camera to capture sharp photos in low-light situations compared to a small sensor.

Crop Factor: The ratio between the size of the sensor and a full frame image.

A small sensor has a lower angle of view and limits frame capture than a full-frame sensor.

Dynamic Range: This represents the ratio from the darkest to the brightest part of an image, ranging from pure black to the most brilliant white.

Since a larger sensor contains larger photosites, it increases the camera's dynamic range decreasing image noise which is a random variation in the image signal.

Larger sensors have many benefits for your final photos but require a larger lens and camera, meaning you'll carry your gear for long periods when taking certain types of shots.

The 35mm or (36x 24mm) full-frame standard sensor size is the largest and comes in both DSLR and mirrorless cameras.

With a full-frame sensor, there's no crop factor, so what appears in the viewfinder will also appear in the photo.

And the combination of a large-aperture lens and a full-frame sensor provides a great shallow depth of field.

APS-H (28.1 x 18.7mm) - "Active Pixel Sensor" is a large sensor available on both fixed and interchangeable lens cameras, has a 1.3x crop factor, and has high ISO capability, which reduces noise.

. . .

APS-C: A trendy mid-range camera and an option for hobbyist photographers who want to get closer to a professional-level camera.

APS sensors come in different sizes.

An example, the Canon APS-C measures 22.2 x 14.8 mm.

Brands like Nikon, Sony, Pentax, and others are around 23.5 x 15.6mm in size.

There are also these types of camera sensors:

The Four Thirds system sensor is for DSLR cameras (17.3 x 13mm).

The Micro Four Thirds system is for mirrorless cameras. With its 2x crop factor, this sensor system is excellent for still photography and high-end video recording.

CHAPTER 10
DIGITAL IMAGING

"I n the world of photography, you get to share a captured moment with other people."
- James Wilson

Digital art is a work that uses digital technology in a creative process.

A scene rendered as initially photographed, with enough processing to make it look its best on screen, still falls into the realm of photography.

However, if the photo contains added or removed elements, it is a digital image.

Digital imaging converts printed text, illustrations, and photographs into digital images using a digital scanner or another imaging device.

Each digital image displays several pixels.

Each pixel is represented on a grid and stored on a computer.

Each pixel's hue value affects an image's color, and the value is encoded in binary code comprising data portions.

The computer reads the information and converts it into an analog image representation.

The pixels per inch influence the resolution of the image.

Resolution: A digital image has different aspects, such as resolution, which refers to spatial detail and clarity, and how much it is possible to enlarge an image without losing quality.

It is possible to predict the resolution through the spatial frequency of a digital image.

A standard unit to measure resolution is the use of pixels per inch.

To get higher resolution, digital artists expand the sample rate.

In addition, zooming in on a digital image allows you to see every pixel.

Pixel dimensions: A digital image's horizontal and vertical measurements are the pixel dimensions.

It is possible to calculate the pixel dimensions by multiplying the width and height by the number of pixels per inch or (dpi).

Pixel dimension's horizontal and vertical disposition help characterize the resolution of digital cameras.

To calculate the PPI, divide the document size by the aligned pixel dimensions.

So, the pixel dimensions of an 8 x 10-inch document printed at 400 dpi are 3200 x 4000 pixels.

Bit Depth: The number of bits determines the bit depth of a pixel, and the bit depth grows as the number of colors increases.

A monochrome image has one bit for each color and uses 0 and 1 to represent black and white colors.

The grayscale comprises several bits of data, ranging from 2 to 8 bits of data and even more.

A color image can have a depth of 8 to 24 bits of information, eight bits for red, eight for green, and eight for blue making up a

24-bit color image produced by combining those three categories.

And a 24-bit image can have up to 16.7 million color values.

Dynamic Range: Refers to an image's light and dark tonal contrast. However, the possible overall tones correlate only to a certain degree.

A digital system's dynamic range relates to its ability to replicate tonal data, which is crucial in digital photography.

High-contrast microfilm had a fuller dynamic range but produced fewer tones.

File size: For storage and sharing, artists calculate the file size by multiplying the document surface area by the bit depth and PPI and changing the file size to bytes multiplied by 8.

To calculate the number of bits in a file, multiply the pixel dimension by each other and the bit depth.

2052 and 3074 are the typical dimensions of a 24-bit image.

When we divide 2,052 x 3,074 x24 by eight, the answer comes to bytes.

Typically, size increments are around 1,024 bytes.

Compression: Standard and proprietary are the two existing compression techniques.

Although most file sizes use a conventional method instead of a proprietary one, the most used techniques are the standard.

However, the proprietary compression technique can retain digital data for extended periods.

Also, Lossless technique schemes can compress binary code without deleting data and is the best option to preserve image files in their original format.

Plus, the Lossless technique removes little information without completely changing the image.

For bitonal scanning, the lossless compression technique is the best option.

File format: It is a standard coded system to store files on a computer; the image and header are bits of information contained in the files.

A file format instructs a computer to open and read a file.

Things like color, bit depth, compression, and metadata differentiate these capabilities between a file format.

Digital Imaging and Digital Cameras: Today, most printed images are digitally processed, and most photographers recognize that doing digital work allows them greater control and precision than older processes, a fact that more traditionalist photographers are unwilling to accept.

Digital Imaging and Computers: For digital image processing, a computer must have four times more RAM than its file size.

For example, to work with a 25MB scan of a 35mm slide, a computer requires at least 96-128MB of RAM.

Since digital image sizes are large, you also need a large hard drive of at least 2 GB that can hold up to 100 MB.

Other file transmission methods are ZIP drives, display cards, and monitor screens.

A graphic card can exhibit around 1280 x 1024 dpi in 24-bit color.

Digital imaging and Scanners: Essential factors in a scanner include resolution and gamma range.

Each scanner controls the software that controls the scans' quality and is the computer's interface.

A scanner that can handle 2700 PPI can make an 8x10 image, and the print will have a resolution of 270 PPI.

A higher PPI means better image quality.

Some of the best desktop scanners are Nikon, Polaroid, Epson Stylus Photo, and HP PhotoSmart.

CHAPTER 11
RAW WORKFLOW

"Photography is the simplest thing in the world, but it is incredibly complicated to make it really work."
                        - Martin Parr

When a digital video camera captures raw data, it records the unchanged data created by the camera's image sensor.

Why photograph in Raw mode? Post-processing is the digital equivalent of developing exposed film in the darkroom. Today, almost all photographers post-process their images in any available raw processing software for maximum control over the result.

In photography, there are three different main file formats.

JPEG, RAW, and TIFF; however, there are some differences between them.

The JPEG file format is suitable for general use and is the most common format for compressing images.

Besides, the JPEG format uses less space on your hard drive and is easier to edit or send through email.

However, due to compression, the images lose some details.

· · ·

RAW files use more space on the hard drive because these are uncompressed files, but they retain all the image data, making them ideal for editing due to their vast information.

The disadvantage of the RAW file is that it is more challenging to edit than a JPEG file.

TIFF files are also uncompressed; like RAW files, they preserve all image data. But unlike RAW files, you can edit TIFF files using Photoshop and retain image quality.

Most modern cameras today offer a setting to shoot RAW or JPEG in their menu system,

Sony cameras use an ARW file format that captures data using the camera's CCD and preserves the data using TIFF specifications.

These files are not compressed and are significantly large.

Nikon cameras use a NEF file format containing all the image information captured through its unique camera sensor.

The NEF is the same as Nikon's RAW file format.

Canon generates CR2 or CR3 files.

A CR2 file has a base on the lossless TIFF format.

CR3 files are equivalent to RAW image file extensions and are closer to CIFF or (Camera Image File Format), which works as a lossy compressed file that is small but has a loss in quality.

Raw files need post-processing software like Lightroom or Capture One before sharing.

• • •

The advantage of taking RAW photos is capturing the best image and the most outstanding detail.

By shooting in JPEG file format, you can save storage space.

The ability to adjust white balance is one of the main reasons photographers take raw photos. White balance is the temperature of light.

The light falls from a bluish cast to warm with a yellow shade.

You can configure your camera to record the temperature of light in a scene. But this can be tricky if there is a mix of light sources or the light changes.

It's much easier to set the camera to auto-white balance and post-processing temperature. Raw files allow you to adjust the temperature of the light. You can match what you remember from the scene or create a mood.

On the other hand, a JPEG uses the white balance selected by your camera.

Most professional photographers choose to shoot raw because this format allows the most flexibility when editing photos later.

For example, professional photojournalists and sports photographers shoot in JPEG when they send images directly from their camera to a media outlet because they don't have time to post-process the photos.

But post-processing is essential for digital photography.

The style and look you can get by post-processing your images will result in unique photographs.

On the other hand, letting a camera do the post-processing by itself will result in a standard acceptable photograph.

JPEG files store 256 color tones, which may seem a lot though raw files can collect even more than 65,000 color shades.

JPEG files take all the scene colors and reduce them by a few hundred. For this reason, a JPEG file is smaller than a raw image, and the format eliminates the other stains permanently.

JPEG images' color tends to appear banding, with shades jumping from darker to lighter because of missing colors.

Raw photos need post-processing.

Fortunately, software like Lightroom can prevent permanent file alteration; however, changes saved to a JPEG file become permanent in other software.

The post-processing software never permanently modifies raw files, so the original file is always there, and you can go back to the original file and start over.

Photos can be made smaller, but it isn't easy to resize an image to make it bigger.

Because Raw photos start larger than JPEGs, you can have many options when exporting the file, and you can make it small enough to post on social media or large enough to print it on a billboard.

Moreover, saved as JPEG, PNG, or TIFF RAW files are easy to share.

Color space, also known as a "color model," is a system that describes color numerically.

There are three central color space systems: RGB for scanners, CMYK for color printing, and YUV for TV/video.

Something worth mentioning about RAW vs. JPEG files is that RAW is a large file and will eventually need some storage space in addition to post-processing your images into a shareable format.

CHAPTER 12
DIGITAL VS. FILM PHOTOGRAPHY

"When you photograph people in color, you photograph their clothes. But when you photograph people in Black and white, you photograph their souls!"

- Ted Grant

In professional photography, film and digital processes and techniques are appropriate options.

The term "photography," literally translated, means "writing with light."

So, light refracted in front of a camera occurs in photography through the lens and projects an image onto the back of the camera.

In film photography, the still image (shadow) passes through a photosensitive material, usually silver, which reacts to light, capturing the image in silver grains of various sizes.

With digital photography, an electronic sensor reacts to light and captures images in identically sized pixels.

Filmed photography was standard twenty years ago.

Then you could capture much higher quality film than on a sensor.

So, most photographers shot on film and scanned the negatives.

As digital camera prices dropped and quality increased, people could take many more photos with much less difficulty.

Today most commercial and industrial applications have gone digital.

Now cameras, with complicated algorithms and programs based on film photography, do much of what film could and are more manageable and profitable.

Unfortunately, now the film is a niche product, and film prices are high.

Meanwhile, digital quality continues to improve.

In digital photography, instead of film, a digital camera has a sensor. Unlike a segment of the film, purchased, processed, and printed separately from the camera, the sensor and the rest of the camera can have an indefinite use.

Most photography today is digitally developed and based on film photography.

From the early 1800s to the mid-2000s, motion picture photography created almost all photographic images. However, digital photography has taken the world by storm today, and everyone, even children, knows how to operate these technologically advanced cameras.

Today a digital camera can easily create a quality image.

A beginner can now do what used to require hours of work in the darkroom and studio with a smartphone.

Even an average camera or iPhone can take pictures that rival the quality of professional film photography of the past.

Besides, one of today's cameras can take thousands of images without needing anything other than a reusable memory card.

Digital cameras can also shoot at extremely high ISO/ASA and can record images that are impossible to obtain with film. In addition, digital cameras often have built-in software that can give pictures specific effects, softening and distributing light in more pleasing ways.

Digital cameras often have settings that help you focus, stop moving objects, compose, and switch to black and white or color.

In general, digital photography has many more advantages than film, and it has profoundly impacted the way we use photography in our society today.

Film photography is a unique physical item transformed by exposure and film development used only once.

Copies can be made from a piece of film by physical printing or digital scanning that come in many sizes.

Film cameras have been in use since the early 1800s in various types.

However, such photography materials have become more expensive and difficult to find.

Still, some people enjoy not knowing what their image will look like right away, while others like the possibility and surprise of the movie. Also, because each shot costs more, many people slow down and create each image deliberately or in reverse, allowing them to play a more prominent role in experimentation and discovery through physical and chemical experiments.

Others prefer the cinematic aesthetic, the tactile and physical experience, the smell, the touch, and the possibility of being away from the screen, things they could not do with a digital camera, even when digital technology and Photoshop offer the potential to manipulate digital images to emulate film.

Now, among the techniques that can improve your digital photography is composition.

Photographic composition is how a photographer arranges the visual elements within his frame since composing a good photo goes beyond focusing on the main subject.

And of the most common composition techniques for photographers who want to create a visually interesting shot is the rule of thirds, which divides frames for optimal composition.

It involves evenly dividing the boundary between two equally spaced horizontal and vertical grid lines, creating a three-by-three grid.

Photography merges three dimensions into two to preserve a sense of space and dimensionality.

Therefore, a photographer must know elements like focus, depth of field, and lines and how to focus them.

Lead lines are visual elements that draw the viewer's attention to a subject or focal point. They can be anything: paths stretching into the distance, an arm outstretched towards something else, tree branches reaching up to the moon, anything that draws attention to something else.

These lines can give flat surfaces the appearance of depth, dimension, and shape.

Focus and depth of field also add to the illusion of a third dimension within the photo.

The shallow depth of field can give the viewer the impression that they are focused on something immediately in front of them and provides an appearance of depth and scale to a plain picture.

Enhance composition with post-production cropping.

If a photo's composition is a bit off, it's often possible to improve it in post-production with a quick crop.

For example, a picture may not optimally frame the subject. But, by moving the frame's border, you can often find a suitable image inside an ordinary one.

When reviewing old images, try looking at them from a different angle or perspective, turning them upside down to see them differently.

. . .

To get the composition right, you need to do more than follow the composition rules for taking good photos.

It is possible to unintentionally pursue things like the rule of thirds or use it without purpose. Understand those composition elements aren't like algorithms or formulas—they help guide a photographer's decision-making skills, not replace them.

The rules of composition of photography are the basis.

However, once you've internalized the basics of what a good image entails, you can break the rules and experiment.

Composition in photography is a tool photographers use to help others see what they see.

They can collect items from a vast world, whether a human-scale portrait, large-scale landscape, or macro photography of tiny worlds, arranging them with expertise.

When you have new ideas for better compositions, you will undoubtedly improve some of your images, and knowing how to manage them is also just as important. In some cases, it will be obvious which technique to use.

In others, putting your subject in the middle of your frame works best. Try techniques like this and see if any work. If not, break the rules and experiment until it looks good.

CHAPTER 13
SHOOTING FILM PHOTOGRAPHY

"*A* photograph is a moral decision taken in one-eighth of a second."
- Salman Rushdie

So much new technology appears every year.

However, many people still feel attracted to analog technology.

Vinyl records are returning, polaroids are gaining popularity, and flared jeans are in fashion again.

And added to this nostalgic list is film photography, which is increasingly popular among professional and amateur photographers.

35mm photo film. The term can mean many different things, but it most often refers to a type of focal length on a lens or film photography format.

A 35mm lens offers large apertures (or f-stops), is versatile, and provides a perfect compromise between a wide-angle and a standard lens.

35mm film, also called analog photography, uses light-sensitive film on cameras to capture photos; an image capture occurs each time light touches an exposed film.

A 35mm format describes a standard image sensor format used in film photography.

A general rule is that the larger the movie, the better the resolution.

Of course, smaller formats like 35mm will be noticeably grainier when printed, but that's often a much-appreciated result of film photography.

A 35mm SLR film camera or a point-and-shoot style are both great for film photography.

Many 35mm cameras have manual setting options, often with automatic exposure.

A camera with automatic settings is best for a point-and-shoot style.

Since film photography is becoming popular, there are new rechargeable point-and-shoot cameras, such as the Lomography Easy-Use Rechargeable.

In general, there are three types of film stock: color negative film, color positive film, and black and white film.

Each roll has between 24-36 exposures.

The color-negative is the most forgiving if you start taking pictures on film, and different film brands inherently have other qualities.

Experimenting and trying extra rolls is the best way to find which ones you like more.

A thing to consider in film stock is ISO.

Higher ISO films, such as ISO 800, are better for low-light photography. However, look for the film at 100 ISO if shooting in bright daylight scenes.

. . .

The way to load your film will depend on the type of camera, though usually, the process is similar.

First, open your camera by pulling the rewind spool up on the back of the camera, where you will load your film.

Put the film in the roll slot, then press down on the rewind spool so that it lowers and connects to your roll of film.

Next, remove the tab at the end of the roll before inserting the guide into a slot on the take-up spool opposite the spool where the film will be wound and pulled for each shot.

Click your camera forward to ensure your film guide loads correctly, then close the camera.

Regarding the camera settings, most 35mm cameras will have an automatic exposure setting, which is the easiest way to take a properly exposed photo.

If you choose to dabble in manual settings, ensure you clearly understand the exposure triangle, which is aperture, shutter speed, and ISO, which can significantly affect exposure and photo characteristics.

You'll be locked to an ISO value based on the used film stock when shooting on film, and your shutter speed will also depend on this ISO. For example, if you're shooting with a Fuji ISO 200 roll, set your shutter speed to 1/125.

Therefore, your aperture will be the setting you manipulate the most to vary your exposures.

One of the greatest strengths of film photography is its excellent dynamic range, especially when shooting in manual mode, because of its outstanding results even when shots are overexposed.

When shooting color-negative film, it's good to set your camera to half or half overexposure since it is much safer to overexpose film photos than underexpose them.

Once you've shot an entire roll, it's time to wind up and

unload your film, and it's vital to properly rewind the movie because light enters the moment you open the camera.

Therefore, incorrect film winding can damage your shots.

Once the film has been shot and downloaded, it is advisable to put it back in a container with a date and location on a note.

Developing a camera film can be done by sending it to a film lab or doing it yourself.

Although the film development process can take time and effort,

is a must for those looking to dive deeply into film photography.

There are also mail services where you can send your reels, such as Indie Film Lab, The Dark Room, etc.

Once you're more experienced with film photography and have even shot a few rolls, there are some additional tips to start experimenting with, such as double exposure, which is exposing a single frame twice or shooting with expired film.

Double exposure juxtaposes two images on top of each other within the same image, adding a new layer of meaning to your pictures.

Shooting with expired film is becoming increasingly popular due to the unique qualities it adds to images, such as minimized contrast, increased film grain, and distorted or washed-out color.

In a way, the expired film adds a nostalgic or aged quality to photographs.

So, whether you're shooting on film or switching between film and digital photography, shooting on film can make you a better photographer.

CHAPTER 14
COMPOSITION TECHNIQUES

"To me, photography is the simultaneous recognition, in a fraction of a second, of the significance of an event."
- Henri Cartier-Bresson

Photography composition is the arrangement of the elements in a photo. A photo has things, and a photographer's job is to arrange them to draw the viewer's eye to the most exciting or significant area of the shot.

Landscape photography is suitable for carefully composing the image before shooting since the subjects are still or slow-moving objects (such as clouds, trees, or the sun).

Additionally, in street photography or photojournalism, a photographer can do the photo composition in a matter of seconds, though, at this point, a photographer needs knowledge, practice, and creative courage.

. . .

There are some essential photographic composition guidelines to help improve the composition of your photos.

Composition techniques in use today were also used in art and architecture since old times; some are essential, and others are advanced composition techniques.

1. Rule of Thirds.

The best-known composition technique is the rule of thirds.

The rule of thirds is straightforward. First, divide the frame into nine equal rectangles, three across and three bottoms.

Many cameras include a function of a displaying grid in live view mode.

The idea is to place the critical elements of the scene along one or more of the lines or where the lines intersect.

The tendency is to put the main subject in the middle but placing it off-center using the rule of thirds will lead to a more attractive composition.

1. The centered composition and symmetry are the opposite of the rule of thirds.

They mean placing your subject in the center of the frame so that it is divided in half, either horizontally or vertically.

Due to the perfect symmetry, such composition creates an aesthetically pleasing balance in an image.

Scenes that contain reflections are also an excellent opportunity to use symmetry in your composition, and often you can combine multiple composition guidelines in a single photo.

Cutout square frames can also be a suitable option for centered compositions.

Symmetry does not always have to be vertical, so reflections can also create the perfect opportunity to capture some horizontal balance.

1. Foreground interest and depth.

Foreground interest applies when the sub-framed element is closer to the camera than the rest of the image, and this technique can create a very intimate feeling besides it adds depth to a scene.

By nature, photographs are 2D, and including foreground interest in the frame gives a scene a more three-dimensional feel and works particularly well with wide-angle lenses.

1. frame within frame

Frame within a frame is another effective way to represent depth in a scene.

Items like windows, arches, or overhanging branches can work it out, and it is unnecessary to surround the entire scene for efficacy.

This way of photo composition presents an excellent opportunity to use your surroundings to be creative.

1 Patterns and Textures

Patterns and textures are visually appealing and suggest harmony. They can be motionless objects such as a series of arches or natural petals of a flower.

These patterns are always an excellent way to create pleasing photo compositions; however, less regular textures can also be pleasurable to the eye.

1. Filling the frame

Filling the frame in a picture, leaving little or no space around the main subject, can be very effective in certain situations. It also helps to focus the viewer's attention on the main topic without distractions.

It also allows the viewer to explore details of the subject, which would not be possible if photographed further away, which often leads to a very original and exciting composition.

1. Using Black and White

Black and white photography removes any distractions from color.

It helps the viewer focus on other aspects of the photo, such as subject matter, textures, shapes, and patterns, and you can use the same composition techniques used in color photography, such as the rule of thirds.

Also, converting a photograph to black and white can be a very effective method of simplifying your composition.

1. Juxtaposition

In art, as in literature, juxtaposition refers to placing two or more contrasting things side by side.

It is a powerful composition tool in photography and refers to including two or more elements in a scene that can contrast or complement each other.

Both elements are more likely to work well and are essential for the photo to tell a story emphasizing the differences or similarities between objects or people.

As with color, shape, and cropping, juxtaposition can become crucial to photographic compositions.

. . .

1. Golden Triangles

The golden triangle composition works very similarly to the rule of thirds.

Instead of a grid of rectangles, this composition divides the frame with a diagonal line going from one corner to another, then adds two more lines from the other corners that meet that line at a 90-degree angle.

The two smaller lines meet the extensive line at a right angle, dividing the frame into a series of triangles.

As with the rule of thirds, the lines (of the triangles in this case) help to position the various elements in the scene.

With some practice, you will soon start using these composition ideas naturally to take your photography to a greater level.

CHAPTER 15
SHADOW PHOTOGRAPHY

"When you photograph a face...you photograph the soul behind it."
         - Jean-Luc Godard

A Shadow can make a scene look dramatic.

Though photography is all about light, blocking some of that light can sometimes add a dynamic feel to a photo; other times, it's unnecessary to obstruct that light to obtain a vibrant feel.

While light is an essential element in photography, shadows are no less important.

Shadows add depth, shape, and texture to a scene, not to mention contrast and balance.

Shadows can even become the focus or subject of an image, and to manage light effectively, we must also learn about how the absence of light works.

In photography, there are ideas to explore to understand and use shadows.

In every photo we take, we capture a combination of light and shadow; however, shadow photography focuses on intentionally manipulating our light source to create shadow-centric pictures.

Concerning a light source, a shadow will change depending on where an object is obstructing that light (high, low, front, side, or behind)

Therefore, we can adjust the angle of the light source and use the light direction to help shape the shadows that appear on or around our subject.

We can also adjust the amount of light and the distance between the light source and our image subject to further improve the quality of light and shadow.

Inverse square light.

There is the inverse square law to incline more into shadow photography.

This "law" means that the intensity of the light source will decrease as the subject moves farther away from it.

This "law" is an effective tool when working with shadows.

It consists of placing the subject closer to the light and then lowering the camera's ISO to expose the image subject while also deepening the shadows properly.

To obtain a similar effect, you can place your subject farther away from the light source and boost the power of the light source, maintaining a lower ISO otherwise, a steady intensity from the light source and a higher ISO would yield a brighter background.

Shadows and silhouettes.

There is a difference between silhouettes and shadows.

In a silhouette, the subject blocks the light to reveal a dark shape against a lighter background.

On the other hand, a shadow is what we create when we use the subject to block light and create a shadowy "duplicate" of an object in the scene.

We can use shadows to create patterns or shapes as another

element of composition to add interest to photos, using them as a subject or in the background.

"Gobos" or (go-between objects)

In photography, gobos use shadows to create patterns or shapes and are one of the most creative tools in studio photography.

A "gobo" describes any opaque, usually black, panel, or "flat," of any dimension between a light source and a photographic subject, as between sunlight and a portrait model.

In photography, gobos work to recreate things that are not in the room.

Some photographers use gobos, or small stenciled circular discs in lighting fixtures, to create a projected image or pattern to add dimension to black-and-white photos; others use them to project silhouettes of designs highlighting abstract ideas.

Gobo pattern

You can use an array of objects as a gobo. For example, you can utilize window blinds and fabrics, among other things.

You can also purchase professionally designed gobos with various shapes and patterns and attach them to your flash unit.

Hard Light

Sometimes when shooting outdoors, photographers warn you against shooting under "harsh" lighting conditions, suggesting you should look after the softer, flattering light of the golden hour.

Whether or not you should follow that advice depends on the style you're after.

Hard light and the edgy shadows it creates work exceptionally well for shadow photography. Remember, a sharp contrast between light and shades can be excellent in this genre.

You can use flash as a hard light source for portraits as well.

Just maintain enough distance between the light source and your subject to keep the light small.

If possible, skip any diffusion modifiers, and place your subject near a surface (like a wall) to capture hard shadows as an image effect.

Aside from studio portraits, landscape, and architecture photography, you can benefit from the hard-light approach more effectively, revealing textures and adding another dimension to the scene.

Experimenting with Light Patterns for Portraits

There are five basic light patterns used in portraiture that use light position and shadows to create distinctly different looks.

Key light positions work for portraiture, whether studio lighting or natural light.

Shadow photography works well in color photography but better in black and white because we can focus more on shadows as compositional elements without color distraction.

Therefore, we focus on contrasting light and shadows when we eliminate color.

It would be better to manually capture the color image and turn it into black and white in the posterior processing or through presets.

We can use shadow photography to minimize the distractions of the scene, lowering the environmental exposure in the camera and carefully placing our subjects concerning the light (natural or flash), which works well in photographing portraits and weddings.

Similarly, if you have ever photographed a reflection and cut it to become the focal point of the image, that reflection becomes the central theme, and the shadow takes the center of the stage.

You can capture your own shadow or focus on the shadows of people or things around them and photograph them.

Additional tips for shade photography

Dramatic lighting after a storm or the quiet morning or afternoon light is an excellent opportunity to capture beautiful shadows in their compositions.

Remember, the shadows will be longer when the sun is closer to the horizon, so if you photograph indoors with a lamp or a flash outside the chamber, the more relative its light source to the surface, it will result in ample shade.

Capturing shadows with your camera in manual mode is a good idea because it gives you more control over the exhibition and the resulting images.

When firing in automatic mode, shadows may come out too light.

Use your camera's LCD screen or histogram to expose the image correctly, and you can always use exposure value compensation (EV) to adjust it.

If a shot is too bright, dial your exposure down to deepen the shadows.

Learning to manipulate and work with light to create low reflexes and lights in your images will also help you capture exciting, varied, and interesting photos.

So, keep your eyes open; You will find many excellent opportunities to include shadows in your images.

CHAPTER 16
LENS CALIBRATION

"No matter how sophisticated the camera, the photographer is still the one that makes it."
- Doug Bartlow

Autofocus calibration is a fine-tuning procedure to find the proper parameters of a photo camera.

Theoretically, autofocus should always produce sharp images when focusing on any subject.

Thus, the importance of autofocus calibration.

1. AF acceptable adjustment methods.

Due to the nature of the phase detection autofocus system on all SLR cameras, manufacturers must properly calibrate cameras and lenses to produce sharp images.

Factors such as manufacturer defects, sample variance, insufficient QC testing/adjustment, and improper shipping and handling can adversely affect autofocus accuracy.

Calibration is becoming a hot topic with new high-resolution cameras like the Nikon D800.

While increasing the megapixels on cameras has several benefits, it can also expose potential focus issues.

A slight focus issue might not be as noticeable on a 10-12 MP sensor, but it will be much more noticeable on a 25+ MP sensor (assuming both sensors are the same size).

While landscape and architectural photographers may not care about focus issues (since they shoot with tiny apertures that hide minor focus issues), portrait, events, and wildlife photographers tend to be more concerned about issues of focus.

Shooting people with wide-open lenses can be challenging to get perfect focus.

If you focus on someone's eye but get their nose or ears? Of course, you want to avoid these problems, so the best is to test your equipment and adjust it for optimal results.

1. Lens Calibration

The calibration process involves going through a specific camera setting that allows fine-tuning the autofocus operation of lenses, which means that we will NOT be changing anything on the actual lens.

Manufacturers are the ones that should only perform physical calibration of lenses to tune and then reassemble the lenses again since disassembling the lens by yourself is not recommended unless you know what, you are doing and are OK with voiding the warranty and potentially damaging the lens.

1. How calibration works

A source of autofocus problems could be a poorly calibrated camera, a lens, or both.

Calibration works because the camera has a setting that compensates for back focus (when focus moves behind the focused area) or front direction (when focus moves in front of the focused area).

Compensation performance goes through small steps, for example, 0 to -20 or +20 in stages of 1, to fine-tune the autofocus system.

Negative numbers compensate for rear focus, while positive numbers compensate for front focus issues.

Negative steps move the focused point closer to the camera.

And a positive number or step moves the focus away.

For example, dialing -5 First means the camera telling the lens: "aim where you would normally focus, except you slightly move the focused point closer to the camera."

This procedure would be necessary when your camera and lens combination is constantly refocusing.

It's essential to remember that the calibration of the camera and lens is something specific, which means that if you have multiple cameras and lenses, you need to adjust the autofocus on each camera for each lens you own (unless you have a camera that constantly fronts or back focuses the same amount in all lenses, in which case you may need to compensate only for the camera.

1. In photography, there is no standard way to name things. Also, the same goes for lens calibration, all brands call things differently for different reasons.

Nikon calls its lens stabilization technology "Vibration Reduction" (VR). In contrast, Canon calls it "Image Stabilization" (IS), and even Tamron, being a third-party lens manufacturer for both Nikon and Canon, chose a different name for the same technology: "Vibration Compensation" (VC). So, all three do the same thing but are called differently by manufacturers.

Some examples are,

Nikon – AF fine tuning

Canon – AF Micro adjustment

Sony – AF Micro adjustment

Pentax – AF Adjustment

Olympus – AF Focus Adjustment

Therefore, be aware of the above naming conventions.

However, lens calibration is available only on higher-end DSLRs because it is an "advanced" feature.

So not all entry-level, upper entry-level, and even some semi-professional DSLRs do not have this capability.

DSLRs with "AF Fine Tune" capability are.

Nikon D7000

Nikon D300s

Nikon D600

Nikon D800/800E

Nikon D4

However, you can determine if your camera has this feature in your manual.

1. Prime and Zoom Lenses calibration.

A recommendation is to calibrate prime and zoom lenses, but there are a few factors to consider.

Most prime lenses, significantly above the "standard" range of 50mm, have very shallow depths of field at close distances.

Zoom lenses are typically much more challenging because there is typically a zoom and aperture range to work with.

A superzoom lens like Nikon 28-300mm f/3.5-5.6G VR can go from 28mm to 300mm, and its aperture changes from f/3.5 on the short end to f/5.6 on the long end.

Calibration is only for a specific focal length when there is a severe focus shift.

If so, pick a single aperture to fine-tune.

To know which focal length needs fine-tuning, go with a focal length somewhere in the middle of the zoom range or pick the most commonly used one. For example, for a Nikon 200-400mm f/4G VR lens, pick 400mm at f/4 for fine-tuning because that's the focal length.

However, for a prime lens like Nikon 85mm f/1.8G, the tuning should be at f/1.8 because it is the most used aperture on that lens.

1. Calibration tools

There are several commercial tools for fine-tuning lenses, and some of them are free.

However, not all free tools are reliable because fine-tuning must be precise to get accurate results.

One method involves using a monitor screen with a test chart image, which can be problematic for proper testing.

Another method is to get a commercial tool like Lens Align from Michael Tapes Design, which is much more reliable and accurate than some free methods.

One last method is to use a semi-automatic software calibration tool to save time and get better results.

Pros and cons of some methods:

DYI Method – Pros: Free, can work if done right. Cons: Precision/accuracy issues take a long time to set up correctly and don't work well with high-resolution cameras.

Lens Align – Pros: Works with any camera/lens combination and can be accurate. Cons: Costs money and requires time for manual adjustments and fine-tuning.

Calibration Software - Pros: Automated/semi-automated calibration process, high accuracy, saving time. Cons: Expensive and only works well with compatible cameras.

1. Calibration steps

There are some recommended steps to follow for proper and accurate camera calibration, and the first step is to identify a focus issue, then try to calibrate the camera/lens, and checking if your calibrated setup works reliably at a different distance.

Identify focus problems.

With an advanced DSLR camera, it is quickly noticeable when there is a focus problem. However, in many cases, the end-user fault or an issue with the camera technique yields soft images,

When a focus problem happens, a tool like Lens Align can help determine if the focus problem is related to back or front focus.

Lens Align and Manual Calibration are straightforward, but being in an environment with plenty of light is preferable.

If that's not an option, you will need powerful lights to expose the Lens Align tool properly,

Set up the Lens Align tool on a light stand or a flat surface, then mount your camera on a tripod and properly level it.

Michael Tapes developed and patented a leveling tool that's easy to use in your camera. Just align the red dots on the back of Lens Align with the holes on the front.

1. Lens Align Alignment

Position your camera a certain distance away, depending on the lens's focal length.

For example, for the Nikon 50mm f/1.4G lens, the recommended distance between Lens Align and the camera is approximately 4 feet.

But you can set your camera at a distance you're comfortable shooting with, but if you need help figuring out where to start, the distance tool can be handy.

Set the AF setting on your camera to "0" AF Fine Tune on Nikon DSLR) or turn it off.

Initially, it is better to start from scratch and go from there.

Focus on the circular pattern on the left side of the ruler with your center focus point, looking through the viewfinder and taking a series of photos.

The focus ring between each exposure would be best, so everything is blurry before you start.

With this procedure, you force the AF system to refocus each time.

Please do this at least three times, then analyze each image on your camera (you can also interpret this on your computer, but it takes time).

If your camera is a Nikon DSLR, zoom in to 100%, then turn the rear dial jumping from one image to another and maintaining the zoom level.

1. Lens Align - Proper Focus

When you get consistently good results using a particular AF adjustment setting, take a few shots outdoors at different distances for a real test run and see if things look good.

If they don't, go back and try the same thing at different distances and see what you get.

Turning AF Fine Tune off is best if you dial wildly different numbers at different distances and focal lengths and don't get good results.

There are other tools like Lens Align. However, Michael Tapes was the original inventor of this tool.

He is the only one with the alignment tool built in because Michael patented it in the USA.

1. Automated calibration

The process with automatic lens calibration is different.

Reikan FoCal is the leader in automated calibration software, performing automatic or semi-automatic calibration (depending on the camera being used or supported), and comes with quite advanced reporting capabilities and testing of each focus point.

The software has recently become increasingly popular on Nikon cameras, thanks to the Nikon D800 asymmetric focus fiasco.

It can clearly show which focus points are accurate and which are not.

Reikan FoCal Nikon D800 calibration process using FoCal Pro.

Automated calibration. PC/Mac Requirements Connect your camera to your computer using the supplied USB cable, turn it on, and install the camera drivers first.

Once the drivers are installed and configured, install the FoCal software, power off the camera, and unplug the cable (for now, until the setup is complete).

Make sure the software recognizes the camera and everything is operational.

The environment must have a lot of ambient light for auto-focus to work correctly.

Print the test chart in PDF with the FoCal software using a high-quality inkjet printer.

Mount the test chart on a flat surface and your camera on a tripod, placing some distance directly in front of the chart, depending on the lens's focal length.

The recommendation is to aim for about 25x-50x the lens's focal length in millimeters.

If you are calibrating a 50mm lens, try around 1.25m to 2.5m, ensuring the graph is parallel to your camera, and nothing is titled. The software will automatically guide you on how to align/rotate the setup correctly.

Connect the USB cable to the camera and your PC/laptop. Then launch the live view and let the software guide you on how to move/align the test target.

Once the software shows you a green check mark, start the automated testing process (Canon DSLRs only).

The camera will take a while to take pictures and adjust focus.

If you have a Nikon DSLR, use Manual Setting Change (MSC) mode, the software will tell you what to change on the camera while you must dial in the values manually.

1. FoCal manual mode

The software analyzes each image and indicates which AF adjustment value works best.

Like the LensAlign process, take your camera for a test run after calibration, take different distances, and see if you get consistently good results.

One significant advantage of the FoCal Pro edition is that it allows you to determine which aperture is the sharpest on your lens.

1. Distance calibration.

A characteristic of the calibration process is that it can vary depending on the distance. And it means that if you compensate your camera for a back focus problem at a certain distance, the focus may drift again if the distance between the camera and the subject changes.

For example, a 50mm f/1.4 lens at 4 feet might require a set of -5. On the other hand, moving the lens 6 feet may require a different setting, say -8.

And then, taking the lens and focusing to infinity may not require any adjustment due to various factors.

First, phase detection DSLR sensors require a lot of light, so all lenses focus wide open no matter what aperture you set them to.

So many variables kick in at once: chosen aperture, focus shift, focus distance, etc.

On top of that, fine adjustments at very close ranges are much more granular than at longer ranges.

The AF fine-tuning system cannot cope with all of these variables.

Therefore, calibration values may differ at focal lengths, apertures, and camera-to-subject distances.

However, this varies on some lenses, and the difference is noticeable, while the differences are too small to be prominent on other lenses.

1. AF fine-tuning remarks.

There are some exciting things about AF calibration on various Nikon DSLRs.

When testing cameras with autofocus issues (with perfectly calibrated lenses), dialing in a value for "AF Fine Tune" would often work for any distance, whether near or far.

Keeping AF Fine Tune at -10 works excellent at any aperture, distance, and focal length.

However, if a camera was perfectly calibrated and a lens had a focus problem, AF Fine Tune would not work as well at various distances.

The worst problems are when both the camera and the lens have problems calibrating the settings, and both give strange/inconsistent results, then more extensive testing will be necessary.

1. Note about camera calibration.

Camera calibration works fine on minor adjustments when the problem is not extreme.

In cases where the camera body is at fault, the impact of an extreme setting is pretty good.

However, this is not very reliable), whereas when a lens fails, dialing above -10 or +10 (significantly above ±15) produces inconsistent results. So, if your camera/lens setup requires high adjustment values (negative or positive), you may not want to mess with everything and send your equipment to the manufacturer for proper adjustment.

That's why no DSLR manufacturer allows calibration for values greater than 20.

1. Calibration tolerance

Anything below ±10 for a camera or lens is acceptable, but anything above will require adjustment by Nikon, and the same is true for lenses.

The autofocus accuracy of your cameras and lenses can change over time.

Accuracy can be influenced by many factors, from drastic changes in temperature to physical abuse and normal wear and tear.

Some people often calibrate several times a month, others a couple of times before and during a wedding shoot to ensure the equipment works as expected.

If drastic changes to autofocus behavior and AF adjustment don't work consistently, Nikon will likely fix it, and this process can be expensive but well worth it.

In summary

Calibration is a complex subject, and many photographers and online resources recommend taking different approaches to lens calibration without understanding how the autofocus system works, leading to frustration for end users.

Knowing and understanding all the process details, including the possible results, is essential before you touch this feature.

Despite all the lens calibration challenges, playing with the camera's AF adjustment feature and learning how to calibrate your camera rig properly is still highly recommended.

CHAPTER 17
CHARACTERISTICS OF LOW AND HIGH-RESOLUTION CAMERAS

"God creates the beauty. My camera and I are witnesses."
- Mark Denman

Photographers often need more clarity about low and high-resolution cameras, asking which camera is better for better photography or the disadvantages or advantages of each one.

The options in cameras today range from 12 to 50 megapixels.

Hence, "low resolution" refers to the minor resolution relative to the highest resolution sensors in full-frame cameras today.

Advantages of High-Resolution Cameras:

The main reason people choose high-resolution cameras is their larger output size, for example, when making a giant print or displaying all the intricate details of an image.

High resolution means more detail in an image on TVs/monitors, the web, and 4K TV screens, equivalent to 8.3 megapixels, and monitors already hitting the mainstream.

And with 8K devices on the horizon equivalent to 33.2 megapixels, we see how high resolution accommodates future technology in favor of higher resolution cameras.

Another advantage is "down-sampling," a resizing technique

known as "resampling," which uses software algorithms to reduce pixel dimensions, helping to crop the image without affecting quality and reducing noise in pictures, and hiding slight focus errors.

In essence, high-resolution cameras mean less noise; in good light, the difference in noise performance between low- and high-resolution sensors is unnoticeable.

Moreover, high-resolution cameras are more efficient for macro, landscape, and portrait photography.

So, for all professional photographers, a high-resolution camera is a must.

Disadvantages of High-Resolution Cameras:

Accessories are expensive, and extra care and maintenance are a requirement.

The higher the resolution, the bigger the image dimensions in pixels resulting in an overall file size that puts a strain on storage, requiring larger memory cards, hard drives, and backup storage, but also on processing power – so it will be necessary a computer that can handle large files at an acceptable speed.

Also, transferring high-resolution photos, copying, importing, and exporting files over the Internet takes time, and large files overload the camera's buffer and sensor.

Plus, high-resolution cameras require high-quality lenses, too, capable of resolving a lot of detail. Older lenses must be improved, particularly when yielding minor detail in image corners.

Lastly, you will use a tripod more often because of the image camera shake.

Advantages of Low-Resolution Cameras:

The price of the camera, lenses, memory card, and other accessories is low.

Also, the files are smaller, making it possible for cameras to push higher frame rates, and they are easy to process.

A standard ram in the computer is enough for post-processing, which is sometimes unnecessary. So, you can continue relying on older computer hardware.

There is also no need for backup storage, less strain in the camera buffer, transfer of files is more effortless, focus error is almost unnoticeable in the photographs, and low-resolution files look better in most cases.

Also, low-resolution cameras work well for sports, wild, and travel photography because moving photography needs high frames per second (fps) for capturing fast action, so quick frame rates are generally preferred over higher resolution.

Disadvantages of Low-Resolution Cameras:

Image pixel dimension is lower, and fewer pixels result in less photographic detail, which can also affect cropping.

Also, images can become smaller than originals limiting the resampling/downsizing/ resizing and spoiling the picture when trying for a poster-size photo.

However, for a professional photographer, the ideal would be to have both High- and Low-resolution camera kits.

In the end, both resolutions work well for different photo categories.

Photography requiring high-resolution cameras:

Landscape photography: is the art that captures images embodying the essence of nature and the outdoors, transporting the viewer, and giving it the sense of being there, witnessing something unique.

Since the usual output is larger prints with more details, high-resolution cameras are a choice in this photographic category.

Architecture Photography: For this category, output size and details are essential.

Macro Photography – Usually done in controlled environments using unique lighting techniques and camera equipment mounted on a tripod.

Frame rates are unimportant, and cropping and printing can be advantageous with a high-resolution camera.

Studio Photography: It also uses a controlled environment to achieve high-quality prints.

Best recommendations for high-resolution cameras today:

Fujifilm GFX 100:

Model: Fujifilm GFX100

Effective Megapixel: 102 MP

Image sensor: 43.8mm*32.9mm, Bayer array

ISO range: 100-12,800

Shutter speeds: 1/16000-30secs

Storage: SD/ SDHC / SDXC

Viewfinder: 0.5-inch, 5.76M-dot, 0.86x Magnification

Image stabilization: sensor shift mechanism.

Dimension: 156.2*163.6*102.9 mm

Weight: 1400g

Hasselblad H6D-100c:

Model: Hasselblad H6D-100c

Effective Megapixel: 100 MP

Image sensor: 53.4*40.0mm (CMOS)

ISO range: Stander: 64-12,800

Shutter speeds: 1/2000-60 minutes (depends on lens type used)

Storage: 16 GB card

Viewfinder: 3-inch (920k-dot)

Image stabilizer: NA

Dimension: 153mm*131mm*205mm
Weight: 2130g

Sony A7R IV:
Model: Sony A7R IV
Effective Megapixel: 60.1 MP
Image sensor: 35.7*23.8mm, Exmor R CMOS
ISO range: 100-32000
Shutter speeds: 1/8000-30secs
Storage: SD/ SDHC / SDXC
Viewfinder: 0.5 type with 0.78x Magnification
Image stabilization: sensor shift mechanism
Dimension: 128.9*96.4*77.5mm
Weight: 665g

Sigma fp L:
Model: Sigma fp L
Effective Megapixel: 61 MP
Image sensor: 36.0 mm*24.0 mm, Bayer CMOS
ISO range: 100-25600
Shutter speeds: 1/8000-30secs
Storage: SD/ SDHC / SDXC
Viewfinder: 0.5-inch, 5.76M-dot, 0.86x Magnification
Image stabilization: image stabilization mechanism
Dimension: 112.6*69.9*45.3 mm
Weight: 427g

Leica M11:
Model: Leica M11
Effective Megapixel: 60.3 MP
Image sensor: CMOS
ISO range: 64-50000

Shutter speeds: 1/16000-60secs
Storage: SD/ SDHC / SDXC
Viewfinder: 0.5-inch, 5.76M-dot, 0.86x Magnification
Image stabilization: NA
Dimension: 10*15*12 inches
Weight: 530g

Fujifilm GFX50S II:
    Model: Fujifilm GFX 50S II
    Effective Megapixel: 51.4 MP
    Image sensor: 43.8mm*32.9mm, Bayer array
    ISO range: Stander: 100-12,800
    Shutter speeds: 1/16000-30secs
    Storage: SD/ SDHC/ SDXC
    Viewfinder: 0.5-inch, 3.69M-dot, 0.77x Magnification
    Image stabilizer: sensor shift mechanism.
    Dimension: 150.0*104.2*87.2 mm
    Weight: 900g

Phase One XF IQ4 150MP Camera System:
    Model: PhaseOne XF IQ4 150MP Camera System
    Effective Megapixel: 151 MP
    Image sensor: 53.4*40mm (CMOS)
    ISO range: Stander: 50-25600
    Shutter speeds: 60-minute-long exposure
    Storage: SD Card/ CFexpress/XQD
    Dynamic Range: 15 f-stops

Phase One XT:
    Model: Phase One XT
    Effective Megapixel: 151 MP
    Image sensor: 53.4*40mm (CMOS)

ISO range: Stander: 50-25600
Shutter speeds: 60-minute-long exposure
Storage: SD Card/ CFexpress/XQD
Dynamic Range: 15 f-stops

Leica SL2:
Model: Leica SL2
Effective Megapixel: 47.3 MP
Image sensor: CMOS
ISO range: Stander: 100-50000
Shutter speeds: 1/40000-60secs
Storage: SD Card/ SDHC Card/ SDXC Card
Viewfinder: 5.76M-dot (0.78x Magnification)
Image stabilizer: sensor shift mechanism.
Dimension: 8.65*8.6*5.9 inches
Weight: 920g

Canon 5DS:
Model: Canon 5DS
Effective Megapixel: 50.6 Megapixels
Image sensor: 36*24mm, CMOS
ISO range: Stander: 100-6400
Shutter speeds: 1/8000-30secs
Storage: SD Card/ SDHC Card/ SDXC Card
Viewfinder: Pentaprism (0.71x Magnification)
Intelligent orientation sensor: yes
Dimension: 152*116.4*76.4mm
Weight: 845g

CHAPTER 18
THE FULL DYNAMIC RANGE OF YOUR CAMERA

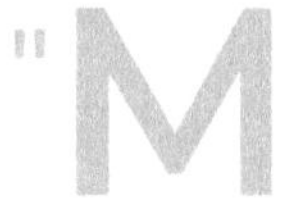

"My job as a portrait photographer is to seduce, amuse, and entertain."
- Helmut Newton

A camera's maximum dynamic range is one of its most crucial characteristics when capturing correctly exposed photos.

Understanding how dynamic range affects the exposure of your images can help improve your photographic ability and technique.

Dynamic range in photography.

Dynamic range is the contrast ratio between the darkest and brightest color tones a camera can capture in a single exposure.

The maximum dynamic range is the maximum amount of light a digital camera sensor or film strip can capture.

Through stops, a photographer measures the dynamic range of the camera.

Each stop indicates a doubling of the captured brightness level.

While the human eye can see up to 20 stops of dynamic range, even high-end mirrorless and DSLR cameras can only achieve around 14 camera stops.

It is necessary to understand how the Dynamic Range works.

To save details in your photos.

Without a tight maximum range, you may choose between turning off highlights (turning the lightest areas of the photo white) or underexposing dark shadow detail (turning the darkest places of the photo black).

A fuller dynamic range lets you capture both bright highlights and dark shadows.

Recommendations that will help you improve the dynamic range of your camera to get a perfect shot.

Neutral Graduated Density (GD) Filter:

An everyday situation encountered by the outdoor photographer is a variation in lighting that exceeds the dynamic range of the film or sensor.

Often a photographer must decide what part of a photograph they don't need, especially in situations where the sky is much brighter than the ground or where strong shadows exist within the photo.

And, with digital cameras, this is even more important to choose from since digital cameras have a dynamic range of less than one f-stop than film, which is one reason to continue using film in certain situations.

The loss of dynamic range for the digital outdoor photographer is noticeable when capturing delicate textures in clouds, giving them a "cartoonish" look. Still, regardless of whether you're shooting on film or digital, the GD filter offers the opportunity to control specific lighting challenges better.

A GD filter is half transparent and half tinted and fades gradually between the fine and tinted portions.

The dyeing can be in various shades of color.

Still, the ND filter is a versatile tool for the outdoor photographer trying to stay true to the scene.

These filters are usually available in one or two f-stops.

The tinted part reduces light by one or two f-stops compared to the shaded region, which does not affect light.

Graduated GD filters limit the luminance reaching the camera's sensor to only part of the image and are a perfect tool for when part of the image is too bright. They come in a variety of levels of darkness.

Landscape photographers find that graduated GND filters work best when shooting a flat horizon, as the filter will also darken any objects in the upper half of the image (such as trees or buildings).

Neutral Density (ND) filters, on the other hand, reduce the intensity of all wavelengths or colors of light entering the camera by measured amounts, allowing the photographer more control when selecting color combinations. . shutter speed, and aperture in a variety of conditions.

Artificial lighting: This is anything that excludes natural light.

Electric luminaires produce and provide the aesthetic effect required in a photography studio or on location.

These include hot lights, which have a warm color temperature, and strobes, which emit a large amount of light in a fraction of a second.

Artificial lighting is easier to control than natural light and is particularly useful when shooting multiple products over several hours, making it more convenient to meet tight deadlines.

You are available at any time of the day or night, so you can be much more flexible when scheduling photo shoots.

The versatility of artificial lighting is a big draw for many photographers, with a wide range of creative results available.

One shortcoming of artificial lighting is the cost involved.

Professional artificial lighting equipment and fixtures are often expensive, which can be daunting.

The installation of artificial lights also requires time, space, and experience.

For some commercial photo shoots, natural light is better than artificial light and vice versa.

The key to taking the best photos possible is determining what kind of light is most appropriate for the specific shoot you're working on.

Adjust camera settings:

Modern cameras have exposure settings to optimize photos in different light conditions, such as night photography or sunlight.

A low ISO setting can also slightly expand the camera's dynamic range to help capture high-contrast scenes.

HDR photography is a post-processing technique that combines photos taken with multiple exposures into a single, optimized image.

To run an HDR photo, take the same photo with multiple exposures to capture the full range of light intensities, then use photo-editing software to blend the images.

HDR is sometimes the only option for producing a properly exposed photo, but its main drawback is that it won't work on moving subjects.

CHAPTER 19
PIXELS AND MEGAPIXELS

"In my view, you cannot claim to have seen something until you have photographed it."
- Émile Zola

It's impossible to read about cameras and have not heard the terms "pixels" and "megapixels."

Today, most cameras are 20 megapixels (MP) or higher, and some even have 100MP.

But what is a pixel, and how many are enough?

A pixel is simply the smallest optical unit making up a digital image.

In other words, a digital image consists of millions of tiny colored squares, each of which is one pixel.

Pixels are the smallest unit on a digital screen.

Even up to millions of pixels make up an image or video on a device screen.

Each pixel comprises a sub-pixel that emits a red, green, and blue (RGB) color, displayed at different intensities.

The RGB color component comprises the range of colors that appear on a computer screen or monitor.

Regarding screen resolution, numbers like 1920 x 1080 refer to the number of pixels, which determines the resolution of a computer monitor or TV screen.

The resolution depends on the number of pixels, the more pixels, the clearer and sharper the image.

Therefore, the resolution of the newest 8K ultra-high-definition TV monitors on the market is approximately 33 million pixels, or 7680 x 4320.

Calculate the number of pixels by multiplying the horizontal and vertical pixel measurements.

For example, suppose HD is 1920 pixels horizontally and 1080 pixels vertically.

So, the total pixel for HD is 2,73,600, Typically displayed as 1920 x 1080 or just 1080p.

The p stands for progressive scan.

For example, a 4K video resolution has four times as many pixels as Full High Definition (HD), and 8K has 16 times as many pixels as 1080p.

Other common screen resolutions include:

480p, or 640 x 480, used in small mobile devices.

720p, which is HD, is 1280 x 720.

1440p, 2550 x 1440, considered a quarter HD (QHD), used for PC gaming monitors.

4K video resolution, meaning ultra-HD, is 3840 x 2160 pixels.

Characteristics of individual pixels.

An individual pixel comprises three colors, red, green, and blue sub-pixel that reacts at different intensities to create different colors.

The specific color information that describes a pixel combines three components of the color spectrum: RGB. And have up to three bytes of data allocated to specify the color of a pixel, one byte for each significant color component.

A 24-bit color system uses all three bytes.

Some color display systems use only one byte, limiting colors to 256.

A bitmap is a light color file that indicates a color for each pixel along a horizontal row, called the x-coordinate, and the same is true for the vertical axis, or y-coordinate.

A GIF file, for example, contains a bitmap of an image along with other data, and each file can support up to 8 bits per pixel with 256 indexed colors.

These types of files combine images or frames to create basic animations.

Each pixel is a square arranged in a uniform two-dimensional grid with a logical direction.

They are backlit individually or by an additional panel; for example, they get lighting through an LCD TV screen.

When the screen is predominantly black on an LCD, only one pixel is light; however, the black panel should still have lighting, which causes normal light leakage on the screen, something you notice around white lettering on a black background on a screen.

OLED stands for Organic Light Emitting Diode, a newer technology for televisions and other digital displays.

Known as "emissive" because it uses millions of pixels that emit light without needing a separate backlight.

They have better contrast, black levels, and viewing angles than LCDs but hurt from burn-in.

They bend or bend and are a feature of modern smartphones.

The physical size of a pixel is relative and depends on the resolution set for the display screen.

One pixel will be equal to the screen dot pitch on the screen set to the maximum resolution.

At less than maximum resolution, one pixel will be larger than the screen dot size, which means that one pixel will use more than one dot.

The megapixel MP.

A megapixel is one million pixels, often mentioned in photography; however, measuring screen resolutions also implies megapixels.

4K is roughly 12 MP, and 1080p equals 2.1 MP.

In photography, megapixels generally refer to the resolution of an image and the number of image sensor elements in modern DSL cameras.

In this way, the camera of the Sony A7 III can take photos of 24.2 MP, which equals 24,200,000 pixels.

Smartphones commonly have 12 MP cameras, while inter-changeable-lens cameras usually range from 20 to 60 MP.

Cameras like Go-Pros or Insta360 can range from 12-48 MP.

First, to understand a megapixel, we need to know that a pixel is the smallest measurement unit used to calculate a digital image.

An MP megapixel is a unit of measurement equal to 1,000,000 pixels, and each pixel is a small square of visual information.

Digital images or videos comprise numerous pixels arranged close together.

Often pixels and megapixels receive the exact quantization. However, using megapixels involves describing the resolution of digital cameras and still images and is also essential for maintaining image resolution in print.

Also, calculating digital video, display monitors, and screen resolution in megapixels is weird.

When scanning and printing images, the pixel count is related to the dots per inch of the scanner or printer.

Characteristics of a megapixel:

1 megapixel = 1,000,000 pixels

Often though, the exact amount may vary in your use of still photography or video.

When a small image looks pixelated or "thick" when enlarged, it means either the image resolution is insufficient for the size, or the number of megapixels is too low.

These days digital photography technology has a more affordable price to buy a camera with enough megapixels to get better image resolution.

And one great thing for today's photographers or filmmakers is that many cell phones come with high-resolution cameras.

PPI and DPI

Pixels per inch, or PPI, express the sharpness of the image on a screen.

PPI and dots per inch, or DPI, are similar concepts and commonly conflated.

PPI refers to the pixels contained in one inch of a digital image.

DPI expresses the number of printed dots within one inch of a printed image.

Differences between PPI and DPI.

PPI expresses an image's digital quality on a screen.

DPI is the quality of a printed image or the number of printed ink dots.

CHAPTER 20
BEST CAMERA SETTINGS

"Taking a picture is like giving a piece of your soul away. You allow other people to see the world through your eyes."
- Katja Michael

Although mastering camera settings is essential, some are overwhelming to understand when considering the names, functions, and camera buttons, dials, and wheels.

So, it is imperative to familiarize ourselves with them to improve the photographic skills of every photographer, even those of professional shooters.

1. The first, and most important camera settings and their function:

Aperture: f/1.8-f/5.6 in dim light or when the depth of field is thin, and f/8-f/16 for a more comprehensive Depth of field.

Shutter speed: 30 seconds to 1/4000th of a second, depending on the scene.

ISO: 100-3200 on entry-level cameras and 100-6400 on more advanced cameras

Camera mode: manual camera mode or aperture priority mode

Metering mode: Matrix/Multi/Evaluative depending on your camera model.

Focus mode: AF-S for photos and AF-C for moving subjects.

Focus area: Single point for still images and Dynamic/Zone for moving subjects.

White Balance: Auto White Balance

File Format: Raw File (or JPEG if you don't want to edit your images)

Drive mode: Single shot for still images and continuous shot for moving subjects.

Long Exposure Noise Reduction: Off

High ISO noise reduction: Off

Color space: sRGB

Image stabilization: On when shooting handheld and off when shooting from a tripod.

HDR/DRO: Off

However often the ideal camera settings depend on the photographic genre and the subject to photograph.

1. Camera aperture setting :

This setting refers to the camera lens aperture, which affects the amount of light that passes through the lens and onto the sensor.

This setting directly affects the image's exposure and is critical to the depth of field, sharpness, and the image's final appearance.

A number known as the F-stop value determines the maximum and minimum aperture.

From this number, we find that the smaller the number, the larger the opening, and vice versa.

In this setting, if you want to have a large part of the scene in focus, you should use a narrow aperture, numbers between f/8 and f/16.

Landscape photography is an example of a narrow aperture, an appropriate aperture for landscape photography would be between f/8 and f/11.

Suppose the goal is to have only part of the scene in focus while other areas of the image are blurry, or the light is dim. In that case, it's best to aim for a wide aperture from the lens's maximum aperture, for example, f/2.8 to f/ 5.6, and this procedure will be the same when shooting portraits and night shots.

1. How to change camera aperture settings:

Typically, the aperture dial is located on the top right of the camera, whether on the front or the back.

1. Camera shutter speed settings:

This setting captures motion and is related to the main exposure settings.

The camera shuttle speed function:

Shutter speed is about the length the camera's shutter is open to capture light.

It plays a crucial role in exposure and affects movement and instability.

The shutter speed measurement involves seconds and fractions of a second in this sequence, the higher the number, the longer the exposure time.

When it comes to shutter speed, to capture movement, such as extended exposure photography, or to shoot in low light, such as night photography,

The correct procedure is to use a slower shutter speed, usually 1/60th of a second to several minutes.

Shutter speed is typically limited to 30" on most cameras, so to increase this time, you can use the Bulb mode setting and a shutter release.

For example, if you take pictures of the Milky Way, the shutter speed is better between 15 and 25 seconds.

However, to freeze motion, you should aim for a fast shutter speed between 1/60 and your camera's minimum shutter speed setting, which is typically 1/4000 of a second.

An example of this camera setting is when shooting action, such as in wildlife or sports photography.

To change the shutter speed setting: Use the dial on the top right of the camera body, either on the front or rear.

1. ISO Photo Setting:

ISO is the last setting in the exposure triangle and the most challenging.

Briefly, ISO increases the light information captured by the camera's sensor, directly affecting exposure and digital noise, thus also helping to prevent digital noise.

ISO levels measure their range following a sequence.

The higher the number, the greater the ISO amount of light and digital noise.

ISO native levels

Ideally, the best ISO setting depends on the size of the camera's sensor and the type of photography.

Under acceptable lighting conditions, a low ISO setting is suitable, and a ISO 100 to ISO 400 can be considered low.

On the other hand, where there is not much light, increase the shutter speed and a high ISO setting of around ISO 800 and ISO 6400.

Set the maximum ISO according to the camera.

For reference, an entry-level camera uses ISO 3200; Advanced cameras use ISO 6400.

1. Camera modes setting dial.

Camera setup for exposure.

These controls allow you to adjust the photo settings for the best exposure aperture, shutter speed, and ISO.

Some setups, such as DSLR or primary mirrorless, require manual camera control.

But only up to a point, as you can benefit from other semi-auto or priority modes.

Main camera modes.

Program Mode P Mode: Your camera automatically sets the aperture and shutter speed in this mode.

Shutter Speed Priority: You set the shutter speed, and the camera chooses the aperture.

Aperture Priority Mode: In this setting, you manually set the shutter speed or aperture for a chosen exposure, and the camera automatically selects the appropriate shutter speed and ISO setting.

Manual Mode (M): You choose all settings in this mode.

Scheduled Shooting Mode: This is a basic camera setting for beginners or when in doubt about which is best for your needs.

Shutter Priority Mode: You can use this setting when you know the minimum shutter speed to freeze motion, for example, when photographing moving subjects, such as in sports photography.

The aperture priority camera setup helps in a wide range of scenarios.

Once you know the aperture you need, such as narrow for landscapes or wide for portraits, this mode will make things easier and is also a predominant mode for shooting wildlife.

The manual is the ultimate mode and the most daunting setup, especially for beginners; however, you can use it in many situations, such as landscape, panorama, night photography, astrophotography, etc.

Use Manual or Aperture Priority mode to take full advantage of your camera's wheels and secure exposure.

All digital cameras allow you to change the camera mode using the main camera wheel or the dial attached to the top of the camera body.

1. Light measurement.

The setting related to camera and exposure is the metering mode.

Metering modes are how your camera measures the light in the scene through the exposure meter built into the camera body.

Understanding how light metering works regardless of the camera mode is necessary.

For example, setting up your camera for a sunny day will be very different than for astrophotography, and how you time the light will directly affect the final exposure of your shot.

If you're shooting in one of your camera's automatic modes, the metering mode will change how your camera adjusts settings.

If you are shooting manually, the exposure value setting (EV) will let you know if the shot is well exposed; also, this setting will change depending on the metering mode.

Primary camera metering mode settings.

Multi/matrix metering: The camera assesses the entire scene's light and splits the frame into different areas.

Center-weighted metering: The camera focuses on the center of the frame to calculate light.

Spot metering: The camera focuses on a point for the best light measurement.

Multi Metering: The default mode on most digital cameras serves its purpose in most situations.

The center-weighted setup is useful for portrait photography, and in some cases, in wildlife shoots,

Spot metering occurs when the subject or area to photograph is slight, such as the eyes in a portrait photo or the moon in a dark sky.

The advanced cameras have direct buttons to change the metering mode, but you must look in the menu for the different functions on most cameras.

1. The exposure compensation dial.

This dial/button also relates to the camera's metering modes.

With this feature, you can increase or decrease your camera's light metering value, letting the camera know that you may want an image overexposed or underexposed.

You can adjust these camera settings even when using automatic or semiautomatic mode.

The exposure compensation dial is helpful in difficult lighting situations, such as when there is high contrast, for example, when shooting scenes in the snow.

Change the exposure compensation dial using a small button simultaneously with a front/rear dial.

Some advanced cameras come with a dedicated button.

• • •

Adjusting the different focus settings, you can get sharp images, and we can divide these into Manual focus mode (M) or Auto-focus Mode (AF) according to the type of photography.

With Autofocus Modes, it's essential to differentiate between camera focus Mode and focus area.

The focus settings in the Nikon and Canon cameras are the same but have different names.

1. Focus mode setting.

After pressing the focus button, the camera locks on, but you can prevent the camera from continuing to cycle through the focus modes tools.

Single Auto Focus Mode: One of the focus mode settings is Single Auto Focus Mode, which locks focus on the subject, but will stop focusing if the subject moves; however, for fixed topics, such as landscape photography, it's a great setting.

Continuous Auto Focus Mode: This is another primary focus setting; once you lock focus, the camera will still try to track a moving subject within the frame, making it an excellent tool for wildlife sports or street photography.

Single Point Area Mode: Manual AF point is the best tool for landscape, portrait, macro, and architecture photography.

Dynamic Area Mode: This is an expansion of the AF point. After you have selected a focus point, if the subject moves, the camera will use multiple focus points to track it.

Therefore, this mode is excellent for action photography.

Auto-area mode: or auto AF point, the camera decides the
focus points to use.

Other focus area setting functions are available but depend on
the camera brand.

When changing the focus camera settings, you will find that
the dials and buttons vary from camera to camera.

1. The White Balance camera setting.

It is a photography set to obtain an image's actual colors without
affecting the light source's color.

The white balance camera setting is critical to prevent images
from getting warm or cool tones.

Also, this setting relates to the color temperature measured in
Kelvins, which means that a higher number on the scale will
result in cooler tones.

There are three types of white balance.

Automatic white Balance: That automatically adjusts the best WB
camera setting.

White Balance Presets: Different preset modes relate to
different color temperatures.

White balance manual camera setting or Custom white
Balance on which you manually adjust the white balance by either
setting a specific Kelvin number or creating a custom white
balance.

. . .

Automatic white balance preset. This setting is best in environments with a single light source and is a default setting in most cameras.

Something you can do when you shoot with your camera in Raw is that in post-processing, you can still change the white balance of your photos.

Most entry-level cameras include a setting to change your camera's White Balance. Still, it can vary from camera to camera except in most advanced cameras, which have customized buttons to change this setting.

1. File format photo settings.

The best camera quality setting is undoubtedly shooting Raw.

Raw files contain accurate original information, which is essential to get the most color and dynamic range from images unless they are JPEG files.

Some cameras can compress and decompress RAW files, but it is better to shoot them uncompressed due to image quality.

Also, if you want to wait to edit photos later, use JPEG; however, SD cards are low on space.

To change the file quality settings, go to your camera's menu, except some advanced cameras have a direct button.

1. Primary drive mode camera settings.

Single Shot: Press the shutter to take the photo.

•   •   •

Continuous or WB: When you press the shutter, the camera takes several photos in succession, and the number of images depends on the camera model.

Advanced cameras can shoot low or high bursts for specific subject occasions.

Shutter Delay: The camera will release the shutter based on the programmed time, which can be 2, 3, or 10 seconds.

This setting is ideal for long-exposure shooting.

Mirror lockup: When you press the shutter button on your DSLR, the mirror flips up to expose the digital image sensor.

Mirror lockup is a feature unique to DSLR cameras that help prevent shaking.

Also, great when shooting from a tripod at a slower shutter speed of about 1/60th of a second.

Shooting at a rate lower than this will result in a blurry image.

To change the settings, go to the camera menu.

1. Extended Exposure Noise Reduction.

In this setting, the camera somewhat reduces the noise in a file.

However, while this process lasts, you can't operate the camera, which takes the same time as the shutter speed.

An example is shooting the milky way for at least 30 seconds, the same time the camera will take to reduce the image noise.

The recommendation is always to have this setting off.

But you can always reduce noise in post-process, for example, by using the Topaz Denoise AI for Photoshop or another version for Lightroom.

Finally, to change this setting, go to the camera menu.

1. High-ISO noise reduction on camera.

So, to reduce noise, turn off the High ISO setting.

Also, noise reduction applies when shooting in JPEG format, and if you shoot in Raw, which is the best photographic way, you can turn this setting off.

You can change this setting from the camera menu.

1. Color space

sRGB and Adobe RGB are settings related to color, sRGB being the most used color space for accuracy among different devices.

Adobe RGB widely manages more colors; however, not all devices can reproduce them.

Instead, they produce weird colors.

Color space is essential; however, when shooting in Raw, you can still adjust color in the digital dark room.

Change settings on the camera menu.

1. Image stabilization setting.

This setting is suitable for handheld shooting at slower shutter speeds.

However, turn this setting off when using a tripod or a stable surface so you don't get blurry images.

In some cameras, you can change this setting from the lens body, on others, go to the camera's menu.

1. DRO and HDR are similar methods that help overcome the problems of indoor photography.

HDR is a computer technique using Photoshop, PhotoMatix Pro, or other software.

However, DRO is a camera technique that is processed by the camera itself.

These two settings aim to create a high dynamic range in the camera.

However, cameras still need to perfect this HDR imaging feature.

Still, a natural dynamic range can be achieved in images by turning off the HDR/DRO in the camera and creating these effects using some software in the post process like HDR Pro or other.

Go to the camera menu to turn the HDR setting on or off.

As a general reference, all camera settings are good, and there are settings for different types of photography.

However, understanding the three main and essential dials on your camera, Aperture, Shutter Speed, and ISO, will help make the most significant impact on your final images.

CHAPTER 21
LENS FLARE IN LANDSCAPE PHOTOGRAPHY

"When the world asks, "what was it like?" Only the photographer can say, "See!"
- Mark Denman

The sun's rays or other light sources can cause lens flares, especially when taking outdoor photos.

This phenomenon happens when the light hits the lens and scatters throughout the system, creating unwanted effects in the image.

Reflections between the glasses within the lens or even imperfections also can cause lens flares, especially in lenses with more elements that are more sensitive to glare.

Have you experienced the strange effect a photograph has when you shoot in the direction of a bright light source?

Those colorful, fuzzy rings that appear all over the image, giving it a soft tint around the frame and breaking up your shot, are called lens flares.

Lens flares can appear in your photos when you shoot day or night.

Usually, the sun causes this effect during landscape photography when the intense sun rays hit the lens, scattering light across the glass.

Of course, these are unwanted reflections between the lens layers of glass which is more likely the primary cause for lens flares.

Another reason for this type of flare that photographers try to avoid is imperfections in the lens.

The positive part is that this effect on the image sometimes adds a tinge of color and a unique and pleasant atmosphere.

Sometimes these effects are present in an image as small rings across the frame or as an enveloping haze and colorless result.

So, if you want to add a soft, warm atmosphere and drama to your image, try this effect.

Some photographers like to add lens flare to their images, and others don't, but luckily, there are some techniques to add or avoid these effects.

However, avoid this lens flare unless you want sharpness and detail in your photos.

A typical lens flare occurs at an aperture closed, typically at f/22 on a wide-angle lens, causing the blaze to appear as rays around the sun.

So, shooting directly in the direction of the light source with a closed aperture will make lens flare more visible.

One way to deal with lens flare is to take an interval of a different exposure when shooting against a brightly emitting light source.

There is also a photographic technique that we need to acknowledge, and it is called Bracketing.

Bracketing is a photographic technique that takes various shots of an image using different settings, resulting in a picture with several variations to combine for the perfect photographic creation.

The most requested type is exposure bracketing, in which the exact image receives three different exposure treatments.

When shooting against the light source, the resulting image will be dark, and often landscape detail will appear null.

On the other hand, when shooting for landscapes or shadows, the image will likely appear bright, and some highlighted areas will also appear blurry.

However, using the bracketing technique, images can recover and enhance the scene's dynamic range.

Now, the procedure for taking multiple exposures using this technique is to expose the highlights at $f/22$, making the light rays too visible.

The next step is to change the aperture to a fuller setting, such as $f/9$ up to a range of $f/13$.

The number of shots depends on your needs for a full dynamic range.

Therefore, the number of shots can vary from 2 to five or even more.

It's vital always to have a cloth to clean around the front of the lens before shooting, as light from the lens can enhance any odd blemishes.

When shooting stars at night, for best results, use a close aperture in the $f/16$ to $f/22$ range, using some underexposure to keep details prominent.

Adjust the exposure times and aperture to capture the full range to get the best possible image. A good suggestion is to set the aperture at $f/10$ and use a slow shutter speed. Take multiple photos to ensure the recording of the full dynamic range.

•   •   •

A bright light source in the background can often produce a beautiful interplay between light and subject.

Taking beautiful photos of the sun's rays depends on various factors, including the type of lens you use.

Some lenses may affect the sharpness of your images, particularly when capturing star scenes at night.

Therefore, choosing the right lens is essential to achieve well-defined star scenes.

Luckily, removing lens flares from photos is a simple process that can be done quickly during post-processing or other methods.

With this information about lens flares, you can improve your photography by knowing when to use it to your advantage and when to avoid it.

Depending on the situation, lens flares can add to the beauty of a shot or detract from it.

By understanding how to incorporate or remove them, you can improve your landscape photography quickly.

CHAPTER 22
LIGHT QUALITIES

"When I take a photograph, I feel that I hold a piece of the universe in my hands."
- Paul Chaplo

Light plays a crucial role in photography as it is what the camera captures to create an image.

Many photographers consider light's properties, including its amount, direction, color contrast, and soft or hard properties, essential in their work.

So, the appropriate amount of light for a great photo depends on the situation and other factors, and to measure the amount of light, photographers use tools such as f/stop, shutter speed, and ISO in their cameras.

The camera's capabilities and settings determine the correct exposure for a picture.

And light sources such as strobes, flashes, LED lights, and tungsten are beneficial and can be adjusted by moving them closer or farther away; however, when shooting with natural sunlight, the time of day is vital in controlling the light.

. . .

Light direction.

Understanding the direction of light is essential when taking photographs.

How the light falls on your subject can highlight or obscure its contours and textures.

Likewise, the direction of the light, whether from above, below, the side, or behind, can drastically alter the outcome of the image. Different light sources can also add an extra element to the look of a photo.

For example, front lighting can be flat, while side lighting can create dramatic texture; however, lighting from above or below may produce unusual results, leading to endless creative possibilities.

Color.

Color is another critical aspect of photography; light color varies depending on the source and situation.

Then midday light tends to be cold and sterile, whereas sunlight in the evening often has warm tones of orange and yellow.

Tungsten lighting can appear orange, while light on cloudy days or in the shade tends to be very blue.

Color is crucial in setting the mood, adding mystery, beauty, and atmosphere to an otherwise dull image.

Contrast.

Contrast refers to the balance between the highlights and shadows in a photograph.

A dominant light source typically brightens the image, and a secondary light source fills in less detailed areas.

Examples of light sources include the sun, a flash, a light bulb, a reflector, or a white background.

The primary light source has the most significant impact on

contrast, followed by secondary light sources that aim to provide equal intensity to fill shadows and enhance overall contrast.

Additionally, bouncing light can also serve as a filling light.

Hard and soft light are crucial in portrait photography.

Soft light, which comes from more prominent light sources, creates less contrast, and is generally preferred by photographers for its delicate appearance.

Conversely, small light sources like the sun produce more contrast and darker shadows, resulting in more intense lighting.

Avoid highlights and shadows in your portraits by moving your subject into a shade during midday shots.

Direct sunlight at the beginning and end of the day is more manageable and provides better lighting for many subjects.

That is, 30 minutes after sunset and before sunrise, an excellent time for low-contrast shots.

Remember to recognize hard and soft light and determine when to use each for optimal results.

A basic understanding of light's main properties—quantity, quality, and direction— helps you fine-tune your creativity.

1. Quantity

Consider the amount of light when taking a picture.

Cameras operate differently from the human eye. While our eyes naturally adjust to the surrounding light, cameras use ISO, aperture, and shutter speed to control the light intensity.

For instance, when shooting in bright daylight, like at a lake, low ISO and high shutter speed or low aperture can prevent over-exposure. On the other hand, at night, a higher ISO is better for capturing enough light.

. . .

The quality of light is more complex than its quantity, and it is measured by visual perception and determined by three essential properties - hardness, smoothness, and directionality.

Also, hard light can create solid shadows and make outdoor portraits challenging.

Moreover, it can also add a dramatic effect to the image.

If you're shooting a scene in bright sunlight at a lake outside while your family swims, your ISO will be lower than at night while your family gathers around the campfire.

Likewise, in that bright daylight, you'll want a high shutter speed or a low aperture to go along with your low ISO, which will ensure that the amount of light doesn't give you a burned image.

The quality of light cannot be perceived concretely as quantity, so instead, it is measured by visual perception.

Complex lighting is intense and directional and can cast strong shadows.

As a result, shooting portraits outdoors is challenging.

However, hard light is not so damaging because it can also work artistically to add a dramatic glow to pictures.

On the other hand, soft lighting is non-directional and tends to come from a diffuse source, but it can create softness and eliminate those harsh shadows often seen under bright light.

By comprehending the properties of light, you can enhance your ability to manipulate scenes and capture detailed images that breathe life into pictures.

CHAPTER 23
PHOTO VISUALIZATION

"Some days, you just get lucky... Other days you wait patiently for luck to happen."
- Destin Sparks

Ansel Adams stated that visualization is a crucial aspect of photography as it encompasses the emotional and mental process of creating a photograph. This term refers to the entire process of creating a photo.

It's worth paying attention to the concept of visualization, given that even a master like Ansel Adams considered it essential.

But how to apply this concept to digital photography today?

For Mr. Adams, Visualization wasn't just a technique but a vital part of the creative process defining visualization as something to consciously project to the final photographic image in your mind before photographing the subject.

The concept means that when you have an idea for a photograph, you should also visualize the final picture and how it will express the feeling you want to convey, considering factors like contrast, color, and sharpness to effectively achieve the desired mood and idea.

In digital photography, there are countless ways to manipulate the appearance of pictures before and after taking the shot.

First, however, we need a clear idea of our desired outcome to maximize this flexibility.

So, the next time you come across a subject or scene that captures your attention, take a moment to consider what drew you to it and what aspects appeal to you.

What emotions or atmosphere do you want to capture?

By answering these questions, you can form a mental picture of the result, which will guide your decisions as you take the shot, then choose the camera settings to process the image.

Having a clear vision of how you want a photograph to look before taking it can guide you in processing the image.

Then, rather than making random adjustments, each decision and action will have a specific intention and direction.

If you want to capture a stunning sunrise landscape, here are some essential tips to remember. To enhance your photo's appeal:

Consider including a combination of clouds and mist in the shot.

When lighting is low, adjust your camera settings to include a 30-second exposure, f/16 aperture, and ISO of 50 to create a slight blurring effect on any moving subjects.

Take a series of two-minute exposures for the best results.

After taking the photos, use Photoshop's sharp S-curve composition tool during post-processing to add depth and contrast to your image. If the RAW file seems uniform, this tool can help.

Adjust the balance to 2.3K to compensate for darker blue light.

. . .

Although cameras and menus are essential tools for photography, it is crucial to understand that the very essence of photography comes from the mind.

The ability to foresee and imagine separates natural photography from technical photography.

According to the late and great American photographer Ansel Adams, visualization is the key to creating a photograph that is considered art rather than just a snapshot.

Therefore, even if it takes time, every photographer should go through the visualization process. For instance, when you decide to take pictures on the main street of your town or in any other place, you are already visualizing the shot in your mind.

If you take the time to explore and expand on this visualization, your photography skills will improve. Sometimes, it only takes a split second to recognize that a photograph could be significantly better if taken from a different angle.

Visualization involves using your mind to direct the shot and the camera before taking the photo.

Walking around and observing the scene before capturing the shot is the recommendation.

Ansel Adams' Half Dome Yosemite photograph from 1927 is one of his most famous works.

He achieved a dramatic effect in his photograph by using a yellow filter to darken the sky.

A common technique used at the time, he also used an unexposed glass plate and a red filter for the desired tones to achieve his photographic visualization.

While photographic visualization is an essential first step in creating a graphic image, more is needed to guarantee a successful final product.

However, it does establish the foundation for the subsequent sequence of steps, making it a crucial element in the process.

So photographic visualization is a combination of imagination and technique, and it involves visualizing the final print in your mind before taking the photo.

It also involves having the technical skills to bring that image to life, even if it's different from the actual scene.

Therefore, the image's quality is vital as the conceptual idea because the two are interconnected.

Visualizing a photo is "seeing" a final color image in delicate pastels instead of bold, vibrant colors and contrasts.

It could mean choosing a particular point of view and then emphasizing the qualities of a foreground object.

But in all cases, visualization leads to which equipment and techniques we need to achieve a particular vision.

The visualization also includes post-processing, where we can visualize a sky or other element lighter or darker than the meter says it should be.

We can skew color relationships and contrasts and plan for interpretive and expressive moods before we press the shutter.

To better understand and capture a scene through photography, consider the mood and attraction of the subject.

For instance, when photographing a large rock, think about how you want to convey the scene's mood - moody, serene, beautiful, or imposing.

Envision the finished picture and the critical features of the scene. Finding the right vantage point is crucial, as even a slight shift in lens position can significantly impact an image's dynamic.

It's crucial to select the appropriate lens.

The position of the lens is relative to the subject.

Therefore, it can result in changes in perspective, such as telephoto "lens compression" or "wide-angle distortion." it can stretch elements at the edges of the field due to the flatness of the film or sensor rather than the lens itself.

When using film or a Leica Monochrome camera, it's essential to consider whether a filter is necessary.

In post-processing, you can reproduce Black and white images, but some effects like polarization and neutral density require a filter.

Refrain from underexpose of essential shadow details in the negative film when determining exposure.

However, exposure may vary for digital and color transparency film.

The world has undergone significant changes in technology and society, leading to a transformation in photography.

The past 30 years have seen further technological advancements, such as a fast-paced society, a desire for instant gratification, and the pursuit of new camera gear.

While traditional photography teachings fade, visualization is now more critical than ever for modern-day photographers, and by mastering visualization and creating compelling compositions, photographers can construct meaningful photographic art.

The advancements in camera and lens technology offer benefits such as automation, immediate image viewing, and accurate metering and exposure.

However, to the detriment of their creative process, some photographers have become overly fixated on technical specifics, such as autofocus speed and accuracy, sharpness resolution, and noise reduction.

The fast-paced modern world also challenges contemplating and creating meaningful photographic works.

The lack of resources focusing on the contemplative aspect of visualization and composition further exacerbates the issue. Therefore, photographers must prioritize visualization and composition skills over technical tools to achieve their artistic goals. Although some authors have written on this topic, there is work to do to restore balance, emphasizing the fundamental visualization process.

Ultimately, artistic vision, light, and technical skills determine an excellent and exciting photograph.

PROFESSIONAL PHOTOGRAPHY

take the same picture twice. First, with my heart, then with the camera."
- Biju Karakkonam

What makes a professional photographer? Is it about making money and living from photography? Or is there more?

The truth is it is not just about profit.

A professional photographer could be called someone who practices or is dedicated to taking pictures and making a living from photography.

So, by the first part of the definition, everyone is a photographer today. But what makes a professional?

Interestingly, the focus is on more than just making money.

It is about a profession's technical and ethical characteristics and standards, and the consensus is that it involves much more than making money.

Hobbyist or professional.

Does a title distinguish a professional from an amateur?

From experience, it isn't.

Some people who graduated in photography do entirely different things.

Besides, some of the best photographers have yet to receive formal education. But, of course, having a degree in photography is fine, though that should not determine whether you'll be a great photographer.

It's daily learning, practicing, developing new skills, and understanding and applying photography theory that develops professional skills.

However, making money from photography doesn't necessarily make one a professional.

Also, a website, a business card, and expensive equipment differ from what makes a professional.

Because in photography, there's always much more to cover.

Quality of work. You can get a chance if you're good enough and willing to improve and learn photography business skills since running a business the right way is also an art.

Let us remember interpersonal skills.

By communicating with people, you're also likely to be successful in photography.

Professionalism is a state of mind, how you approach your job, and the effort you put into educating yourself.

It is the self-motivated learning you do at the beginning and throughout your career.

Also, professionalism is the amount of research you do before taking the photo, and more importantly, it's about the relationships you build.

There are a lot of criteria to meet to be called a professional, and being a professional photographer goes far beyond making money.

It involves more than mastering a camera or owning the best equipment, like a Sony Alpha a7 IV, Leica Q2, or Panasonic Lumix GH6. Still, the inherent qualities are to see beauty in the most unexpected places and capture the beauty in a shoot.

· · ·

There are types of photography, each with different exacting standards; a pet photographer must know how to interact with animals appropriately; Sports photographers need to be fast, strong, and able to improvise to get the best shots.

Some desirable qualities to have in photography may be creativity and imagination.

Great photography requires a creative mind and a lot of imagination to look at something ordinary and find different ways to make it look extraordinary in a beautiful and meaningful photograph.

As you may know, composition in photography is everything.

So even if you're not concerned with the artistic side of your craft, photo composition is still crucial in producing great photos.

Composition rules can help the photo artist, but in the end, creativity with imagination to manage lighting and storytelling takes a photo stand out.

In photography, examining minor details is critical to producing the perfect image.

However, sometimes things turn out differently than expected, and there will be times when you must take a billion photos to get that perfect shot.

In any field of photography, patience is an essential quality, even when waiting for the perfect lighting.

Besides being patient, a photographer must be flexible to make the most out of undesirable conditions to gain clients and partnerships.

Knowing how to interconnect with others effectively is imperative when photographing people.

Though it takes a lot of time and effort to succeed, a passionate photographer always shines through his work and is willing to learn and improve continually.

Acquiring technical skills is just the beginning. For example, a good photographer also needs artistic vision and storytelling skills. These all take time to develop but will soon become second nature.

It is essential to train the eye to see the world as "pictures" and to observe fine details even when you do not have a camera.

You need to be curious and go beyond the obvious. Great photographers can find something unique and beautiful in the most ordinary scenes. They are always looking for stories and new ways to capture them for their audience.

Like everyone else, photographers have different lives and professional circumstances, but each must follow their path.

Before pressing the shutter, some know what they want and how to say it, while others need to enter the art world, take photography classes, study the work of photography masters, and practice long before they reach their destination.

The struggle is not learning to manipulate a camera or choosing lenses and locations.

Instead, the hard work of photography is finding something that speaks to you and motivates you to pick up a camera, connect with your subject, and create meaningful photos while enjoying the process.

Once you know the skills, you can start exploring the personality traits of a photographer.

Remember that the first quality you must have is patience because sometimes things turn out differently than planned, and you must find the strength to keep going.

Therefore, focus on developing patience, resilience, adaptability,

and a healthy dose of communication and management skills.

It would help if you learned to negotiate respectfully and knew when to give in and when to defend your artistic purpose.

A good photographer finds the best way in any situation, even when the case is unexpected.

CHAPTER 25

REQUIREMENTS FOR A STUNNING PHOTO

"The eye should learn to listen before it looks."
- Robert Frank

The requirements for a fantastic picture are diverse, and all work together in the composition of a great photograph.

Among these requirements are the lighting factor, the knowledge of the rule of thirds, shapes, textures, patterns, color management, and more.

Have a vision.

There must be a reason for a specific type or photo style, whether a fleeting image, a family snapshot, or the most remarkable piece of art ever created.

It would be best to have a vision behind a photograph.

For example, when the shoot is about the landscape, the consideration for a unique picture could be the mood and availability of light in the area and the best way to achieve such an image.

A helpful technical procedure can be first to watch the image in mind, identifying the message or emotion you are trying to capture.

Then approach all photography aspects consciously.

Every bit of the photo should intentionally look to transform your unique subject.

Discovering an Inspiring Topic.

Occasionally, a topic we enjoy may not be ideal for sparking creativity. However, exploring a particular mood or emotion in our thoughts can be valuable and lead to a fulfilling experience.

Choosing the right subject for our photos requires careful consideration.

We must remember that each subject is unique, but sometimes it may not align with our initial idea.

While most subjects are great, some may suit specific goals. Therefore, we must choose our topic with intention and purpose. Ultimately, every photo we take reflects our imagination and the reason behind our actions.

When taking photos, it's essential to evaluate the elements in the scene and avoid anything that doesn't fit your ideal subject or background.

Post-processing can minimize unwanted features in your photo. Additionally, consider changing the layout by adjusting your position or using different lenses.

A well-positioned camera can save time and contribute to an overall better image look.

To ensure quality pictures, always take photos with a purpose and pay attention to every place and environment to discover great subjects to work with.

Photography reaches its highest level when the entire image is deliberate and appealing to the viewer. Any unnecessary elements in the picture will detract from its meaning. Conversely, a purposeful vision will naturally align with someone's search.

Every photo you take has value and can be just what someone is searching for.

Whether or not someone loves your picture depends on what they're looking for and the mood and personality you add to each photo as a photographer.

However, it's essential to enjoy what you're photographing first and foremost; then, everything else will fall into place for both you and the viewer.

This principle applies in most cases and when capturing the best mountain, landscape, or portrait photo.

Ultimately, the viewer's taste decides if your photo is unique because of its beautiful and distinct attributes.

Any dark, moody, or calm photo can be the most beautiful photograph for the right person, whether it's a sunrise or sunset or when very little light remains and much of the subject is in shadow.

It's impossible to know exactly how others will perceive your images. However, audiences tend to appreciate artistic creations that are beautiful and interesting.

Therefore, what you find attractive will likely also attract your audience, also generally, the photographer and viewer have similar perspectives on beauty with some minor differences.

If you don't have a specific target audience, create, and share photos that reflect your style.

This approach will typically attract the right audience and earn their admiration.

An image with a clear purpose and impactful expression is likely to capture viewers' attention.

While various elements of photography, like light, composition, and subject, are essential to achieving a vision, a great photo can always successfully appeal to diverse tastes.

When taking photos, it is essential to have a clear purpose.

You can achieve this by selecting a specific subject and ensuring that every aspect of the picture serves a purpose.

Remember, great photos are not accidental but a result of intentional and well-planned shots.

Keeping this in mind will help you improve your photography skills.

CONCLUSION

"For me, the camera is a sketchbook, an instrument of intuition and spontaneity."
- Henri Cartier-Bresson

Professional photography involves refining one's craft to capture various moods and creations with technology.

Like painters, photographers continually analyze new concepts and techniques to enhance results.

Once a photographer has a firm grasp of the fundamentals of photography, they can explore more advanced topics such as elemental composition and technical aspects like ISO invariance and selecting the sharpest aperture, among other photographic elements.

Although advanced photography may not appear essential for taking good pictures, professional photographers constantly strive to improve their skills.

Photographers who are artists can express their expertise through images. Thanks to digital technology advancements, taking photographs has become more accessible in the art world, and today pictures have a comparable impact as other art forms.

Once you have reached a better understanding of photography, it's natural to progress towards more advanced and intricate techniques with your camera, whether it is an SLR or digital.

Let's keep taking photos because photography is not just a skill or hobby but a passion that can fulfill our creativity.

And keep exploring different techniques to capture captivating images.

Hoping this book serves you well and brings you many joyful photography moments and experiences.

A Gabriel P